To my friends + pupils:

I hope this book will help
you to enjoy life, and the great
game of golf to its' fullest.

Sincerely
Harvey Penick

And If You Play Golf, You're My Friend

FURTHER REFLECTIONS OF A GROWN CADDIE

Harvey Penick
with Bud Shrake

SIMON & SCHUSTER

New York   London   Toronto   Sydney   Tokyo   Singapore

SIMON & SCHUSTER
Rockefeller Center
1230 Avenue of the Americas
New York, New York 10020

SIMON & SCHUSTER and colophon are registered trademarks
of Simon & Schuster Inc.
Manufactured in the United States of America

5   7   9   10   8   6

Library of Congress Cataloging in Publication Data

Penick, Harvey.
And if you play golf, you're my friend : further reflections of a
grown caddie / Harvey Penick with Bud Shrake.
p.   cm.
1. Golf—United States—Anecdotes.   2. Golf—Study and teaching.
I. Shrake, Edwin.   II. Title.
GV965.P413   1993
796.352′0973—dc20   93-33056
CIP

ISBN: 0-671-87188-9

"If you read my books you're my pupil, and if you play golf you're my friend."

HARVEY PENICK
Golf Professional Emeritus
Austin Country Club
Austin, Texas, 1993

Contents

My Son-in-Law's First Lesson   17

Teaching Billy   18

A Value of Knowledge   21

Identify the Problem   21

The Lawyer   22

God Knows   28

In the Mind's Eye   28

What Does It Mean?   30

Take Pleasure in It   31

Flavor That Lasts   32

The Oracle Speaks   32

A Story by Helen   35

Another Call   36

Toss It   37

An Irony   39

The First Choice   39

A Strange World   40

Look Here First   40

Toward a Stronger Grip   41

All You Need to Know About the Wrist Cock   44

Higher Aspects   45

A Method for Madness   47

Making a Comeback   48

A Distinction   52
Preacher Mann   53
The Reason for It   54
From the Fringe   55
South of the Border   55
The Lay Up   59
Tommy Wins the Open   59
A Story by Christy Kite   62
Make Up Your Mind   63
The California Woman   65
The Judge   67
Keep It Moving   68
The Learning Game   69
A Story by Tom Kite   70
The True Way   71
Club Selection   72
A Special Club   73
A Golfer's Prayer   75
Give Luck a Chance   76
The Bench   78
A Teacher's Guide   79
Musings on Rulings   85
Wilmer's Woes   87
The Power of Negative Thinking   88
The Champion   89
Practice It First   90
Wrongheaded Husbands   91

Children   92
Crosshanders   92
The Left Arm   95
The Secret of the Golf Swing   96
Hit It Hard   97
Brand-Name Aiming   98
Slices and Hooks   99
Pressure   101
The Erratics   104
How to Stop the Bleeding   106
The Dashing Demaret   108
Luck   109
Sweet but Incomplete   110
Paula Granoff's Story   111
Indoor Teaching   118
Masters Manners   120
A Golfer's Poem   121
Wasting Your Time   121
Mr. Connerly   122
Fate Takes a Hand   124
Unfair to Ben   127
Made in Heaven   128
Chipping   128
What Do You Look At?   130
Telephone Lesson   131
Still the Most Dreaded Shot   132
Reassurance   134

A Future in Golf 135

The Sweet Spot 138

Playing Hurt 140

The Feeling of Far 142

In the Eyes 143

In the Mind 144

Old Familiar 145

Governor Hobby 146

Life in the Mind 147

My First Lesson 148

A Soft Wedge 149

The Examination 150

Club Fitting 151

The Best Hands 152

A Hard Job 154

Mr. Aminex 154

An Inexhaustible Subject 155

A Tip 156

The Fee 157

Timing 158

Time to Move 159

Mr. Roberts 160

Randy's Driver 161

Jack Did It 162

The Downhill Lie 163

Haunted 164

Hogan Whiffs It 165

Caddie-Yard Psychology   167
Where Is He?   168
My Prayer   168
Training Aids   169
Necessity   171
Summing Up   171
Game of Honor   172

And If You Play Golf, You're My Friend

My Son-in-Law's
First Lesson

MY SON-IN-LAW, Billy Powell, was captain of the University of Texas basketball team. When my daughter, Kathryn, married him, Billy's pals accused him of trying to improve his golf game.

Everybody knew that was meant as humor, because Billy had never touched a golf club. Basketball was Billy's idea of a real game, not golf.

After college, Billy and Kathryn served a tour in the Air Force. They were stationed at Clovis, New Mexico. Billy tried golf for the first time in Clovis. Playing with a friend who had a 2 handicap, Billy learned what a thrilling experience golf can be. He was hooked.

Billy phoned me that night. He was so excited, he could hardly catch his breath.

"Harvey, I'm on my way to Austin to take a lesson," he said. "How soon can you fit me in?"

I said, "Billy, I will send you a set of golf clubs. Play golf for six months. Then we'll talk about lessons."

Six months later, Billy and I went to the practice range at Austin Country Club.

"I have to ask you a question," Billy said. "I've had an awful struggle for six months. Why did you make me wait so long for this first lesson?"

"This is the second lesson," I said. "Your first lesson was six months of struggle on your own."

"But why?"

I said, "Athletes like you, who have had success in other sports, need to be humbled before they can learn the game of golf."

There's an old saying: The student must be ready for the teacher to appear.

Teaching Billy

I WATCHED MY son-in-law swing at the ball on the practice range for a while without comment. I could tell he wanted me to say something.

Finally I said, "Billy, if you handled your fork the way you do that 7-iron, you would starve to death."

We set the ball on a low tee.

"Now take a swing and just clip off that tee," I said.

He hit behind it. He topped it. He hit it sideways.

I said, "You're a good athlete. Learn to clip off that tee. We can go no further until you do."

I left him alone on the range.

He swung his 7-iron for two days before he learned to clip off the tee.

As our lessons progressed, Billy was eager to reach for the driver. Like everyone, he wanted to boom that ball 250 yards down the fairway. But try as he might, every drive was a slice.

"You'll never get the full enjoyment out of this game hitting a slice," I said. "The only thing that can happen to a slice is, it will get worse."

I took away all his wooden clubs and his long irons. I told him to hit a 4-iron off the tee when he played golf. As soon as he learned to hit a consistent hook off the tee with his 4-iron, we would think about using the wooden clubs.

Months passed. At last Billy's hook was pronounced. He was certain he was ready for the driver. "I can hook my driver now, I believe," he said.

He showed me he could hook it all the way into the trees.

I reminded him that the rough on the left of the fairway is as bad as the rough on the right.

"By the way," I said, "only use your 1-iron when you are in the woods either right or left."

"Why is that, pro?"

"Because you might break it, and then you won't be tempted to use it anymore. I want you to lock your driver, 1-iron, and 2-iron in the closet. Hit your 3-wood off the tee. The more loft you use, the better you will keep the ball in play."

Billy didn't want to hear this, and he didn't obey. He kept trying to hit the ball long distances with his driver. It held his scores back for several years.

Meanwhile, I was constantly trying to help Billy with his putting stroke. Nearly all pupils return to their original sins in the putting game. Billy's original sin was a short backstoke and a long follow-through.

Every time Billy came to Austin I would say, "Let's see your putting stroke." And there it would be—short back, long through. We would go to the practice green and putt until his back and forward strokes were the same length.

It has been nearly forty summers since the day I gave Billy his "second" lesson, the one that followed his six months of learning humility. Billy became a pretty fair player at Levelland Country Club in West Texas, where he and my daughter, Kathryn, have lived for many years. Billy was the first basketball coach at South Plains College—and the golf coach, as well.

Recently, Billy visited me as I sat under the trees at Austin Country Club on a warm, sunny morning.

"Let me see your stroke for an imaginary two-footer," I said.

You guessed it: Short back, long through.

"Billy, you would have knocked that one off the green," I said. "We better go watch you stroke a few."

A teacher's job is never finished.

A Value of Knowledge

I HEARD BARBARA JORDAN say her grandfather told her that people would reward you, employ you, and pay you if you know how to do something. He encouraged her to learn, and said people would give her an opportunity regardless of color if they respected her knowledge.

As a grown caddie with a high school education, I spent my life learning golf and how to teach it. Barbara Jordan's grandfather was right. People have come to me from all over the world seeking the use of my knowledge, humble though it is.

Identify the Problem

BILLY MUNN, one of my better college players, came into the golf shop at Austin Country Club and said he was putting poorly. He asked if I would help.

When we left the shop, Billy walked toward the practice green and I walked toward the practice range.

He thought I had misunderstood.

"Hey, Mr. Penick!" he yelled. "It's my putting that needs looking at!"

"Billy, you're a good putter," I yelled back. "If you aren't having success, it's because your iron shots are too far from the hole."

The Lawyer

HE WAS A LAWYER, about sixty years old, a 14 handicap from another club in town. Over the past thirty years I had given him three or four lessons. Lawyers are not keen on taking lessons. Like engineers and accountants, they want to analyze and complicate everything.

"Harvey, here's my problem," he said. "I've been in a courtroom on a tough case for the last seven weeks. On Saturdays and Sundays, I was reviewing and planning. In preparing for the trial, I worked day and night. This morning, the jury voted for my client."

"Good work," I said.

He nodded. "The problem is, I'm going to Florida to play in a member-guest with an old friend. I haven't touched a golf club in three months. I don't want to embarrass myself or my friend in Florida. Will you watch me hit a few?"

"When does your tournament start?" I asked.

"Tomorrow."

"Tomorrow?"

"I have a flight early in the morning. Our practice-round tee time is 1:47."

I suggested we head for the putting green. "Chipping and putting will get your mind back into the game faster. If you can get up and down for pars a few times in Florida, it will make your friend happy."

"Actually, I'm a pretty good putter," the lawyer said.

On occasions when he had played at our club as a guest, I had heard the lawyer's friends kidding him about his putting, and not because he was so good at it. We reached the practice green. I selected a level, straight ten-foot putt and asked the lawyer to put down three balls.

The best way to sharpen your putting is to practice with one ball, just as if you are playing that hole on a golf course. But the lawyer was rusty from months away from the game. He needed to get a feel for how far his ball would roll. By using three balls we could see how his touch was adjusting.

"Stop a minute," I said after he had lined up the putt from behind the ball and taken his stance. "Where are you aimed?"

"I don't know."

"Try bringing your right foot back to the line and squaring up."

"I like this open putting stance. I feel more comfortable," he said.

And he knocked that first ball straight into the cup.

"See? I can see the line better with my shoulders open."

"Hit me another," I said.

The second putt missed the hole by inches and went

12 feet past. The third putt was two feet short and wide right. This lawyer didn't have any touch at all on this day. His putting stance was so open—maybe he thought he was copying Raymond Floyd, but it was so exaggerated that it had become a burlesque—that it allowed him no real conception of where his putter was aimed.

We fetched my briefcase and set it on the green, handle up, directly along the line of the putt.

"Please stand square to my briefcase," I asked. "Make some practice strokes. I want the toe of your putter to brush my briefcase. But don't scratch the leather."

"This feels so awkward," he said.

That is always the reaction of a person who plays from an open stance and doesn't understand what square is. "Now let's try it with a ball," I said.

He made two out of three putts, just by my briefcase forcing him to keep his putter face square. Not scratching the leather gave him something to think about, and that produced a good stroke.

We moved to chipping from the fringe with a 7-iron. It would be best for him to stick with one chipping club for a while. I persuaded him to stand close to the ball, not reach out for it. Play it off his right toe, feet close together. I asked him to pretend he was chipping the ball under a bench. He did all right, so we moved to the practice tee.

As usual, I asked him to bring his 7-iron and his 3-wood.

"Harvey, I need to hit some drivers," he said. "There's some swamps in Florida that I can't carry off the tee with my 3-wood."

I remembered that by using the "clip the tee" and

"work by the hour" images with this fellow years ago—once I had squared his hips and shoulders with a touch of my cane—he had begun to hit such beautiful 3-woods that he cried out with joy, and I got goose pimples on my arms.

"We'll come to the driver soon enough," I told him. I didn't tell him that soon enough would not be today. "First, hit me some 7-irons."

The lawyer made a few practice swings, slow and lazy. He looked pretty good. He seemed more interested in his swing looking good than in anything else. He thought so intently about how his backswing and his follow-through looked that he almost forgot the part in between. He forgot about clipping the grass with his practice swings. He forced his swing to look good, and the effort kept him from having good balance.

"That's plenty of practice swings to make for a tournament that starts tomorrow," I said. "Maybe you better start hitting some balls."

With a slow, weak effort he flailed the ball about 100 yards.

"Got to loosen up the grease," he said.

"Let's hit this next one hard," I said.

If anything, the swing was even weaker.

"See that flag down by the rock? Take dead aim on it and hit the ball hard."

He made a nice, smooth, rhythmical swing that was the least powerful movement he had made yet. The ball landed short of the rock that was about 120 yards away. The lawyer's club didn't hit the ground hard enough to take a divot.

"That looked pretty good, didn't it?" the lawyer asked.

"Your swing is so weak, if you had been hitting my foot with that 7-iron you wouldn't have bruised my toe," I said.

A sarcastic tone had crept into my voice. I wish it hadn't; a teacher can say almost anything and not offend if he uses the right tone of voice. I should have laughed as if I were joshing him.

The lawyer was more surprised than offended.

"Why, Harvey, I'm sort of stiff. I'll warm up in a minute. I'm not gonna hit you in the foot to prove it, either."

"I shouldn't have spoken to you like that. Hit the rest of those balls," I said. "I'll just keep quiet."

While the lawyer was gently lofting weak, slicing 7-irons, I slipped away.

I hid behind the bushes at the rear of the practice tee. By peeking through some leaves, I could see the lawyer.

"Where did Harvey go?" the lawyer asked.

"I don't know. Didn't see him leave," a member said.

"Does he often vanish in the midst of a lesson?" asked the lawyer.

"He's been known to do it before, yes," the member said.

The lawyer looked at the pile of balls at his feet. He decided he might as well hit them, no matter if I had disappeared.

I watched him through the bushes for fifteen minutes.

What could I tell this lawyer that would help him play in the tournament in Florida?

He needed to square his hips and shoulders. He needed a stronger grip. He needed to stop his left wrist from breaking down.

26

Had this pupil been a good player, I could have showed him any or all of these things. But any advice I would give the lawyer about his stance and swing would make him worry about it on the plane, and then he'd overdo everything.

So I went home.

I sat in my chair and thought about the lawyer. There must have been some way I could help him. I believed I had helped his putting stroke. We had kept his hands ahead of the clubhead by chipping low shots under the imaginary bench. As he kept hitting those weak, slicing 7-irons—he called them "fades"—I noticed that he was consistent with them. It was a shot he could count on. A person can build an entire round around one consistent shot.

Finally, about dinner time, I asked Helen to phone the lawyer.

"Hello, this is Helen Penick," she said. "Harvey asked me to call. He can't hear well enough to talk on the phone, you know. Well, he has been sitting here for hours thinking about you. And he said for me to tell you this—go to Florida and have a good time, you'll do just fine."

Two weeks later he came by the club to see me. He was a happy lawyer. He and his friend had won their flight, and he had shot his handicap. He thanked me for helping him tune up his swing.

I should have thanked *him*—for reminding me that it's not what the teacher says, but what the student hears that matters.

God Knows

GOD MADE WHAT is called the lifeline in the right palm of a human being for one very special reason . . .

It fits just exactly perfectly against the left thumb in a good golf grip.

In the Mind's Eye

BARBARA PUETT APPROACHED me one fine spring morning with a problem that was confounding her.

"Harvey, I'm hitting it fat," she said. "No matter how I adjust, I keep hitting behind the ball. I'm desperate. Please tell me what's gone wrong with my swing."

Barbara was one of my better pupils. She used to play round after round with young Tommy Kite. By the time Barbara came to see me with this "fat" problem, she had become a golf teacher herself.

"Let me watch you hit a few 7-irons, Barbara," I said.

She made a few swings. Sure enough, she hit behind the ball every time. Barbara's address position looked fine. She was too good a player to be doing this.

"Let's not use a ball," I said. "I want you to pick out a spot on the ground, a leaf or a piece of grass, and hit that spot."

"I'll try," Barbara said.

She would select a leaf or a twig or a tuft and swing at it—and her 7-iron would dig into the ground behind it. Barbara was growing very upset.

"What's wrong with my swing, Harvey?" she pleaded.

"I can't say," I said.

"Why?"

"Barbara, after all the years you've spent practicing and playing golf, if you can't hit a spot on the ground with your swing, there is nothing I can do to help you. Go home. Go out in your backyard. Keep swinging your 7-iron at a spot on the ground. When you hit that spot regularly, come back and see me—if you need to."

The next time I saw Barbara she had just finished a round of golf and turned in a good score. She was excited.

"You cured yourself," I said.

"I went to my backyard like you said. I started swinging at a spot," she said, grinning, "and suddenly it came to me.

"There was nothing wrong with my swing. If I couldn't hit a spot, it was because my mind wasn't on it. Once I quit thinking about my swing and really put my mind onto hitting a spot, the problem went away."

What Does It Mean?

EVER SINCE Ben Hogan's book, *Five Lessons: The Modern Fundamentals of Golf,* was published in 1957, hardly a week has gone by without at least one pupil wanting to engage me in a discussion about "pronation" and "supination."

Usually it begins with the pupil asking, "What do 'pronation' and 'supination' really mean, anyhow?"

The actions indicated by those words have been a natural part of the golf swing since the game began. Seymour Dunn, a Scot from North Berwick, wrote what he called a "scientific explanation" of pronation and supination in a book published in 1922. My son, Tinsley, and I used to study the photographs in Dunn's book when Tinsley was a boy.

But the average golfer had never given a conscious thought to pronation and supination until Hogan's book—written by Herbert Warren Wind and illustrated by Anthony Ravielli—captured the public fancy.

I stay away from those words in my teaching.

But to answer the question of what they really mean, as simply as possible, this is what I say:

"My dictionary says pronation is turning the hand so the palm faces downward. Supination is turning the hand so the palm faces upward. Now forget about those words, and let's get back to golf."

Take Pleasure in It

I WAS INVITED to be honorary starter at the Texas Women's Amateur championship when it was played at the Barton Creek Club. It was a thrill to be wanted by so many women.

As the first morning matches were setting off, one of my Austin Country Club friends and pupils, Carrell Grigsby, came over and knelt beside my golf cart and held my hand.

I could feel in her grip, and see in her eyes, that Carrell was nervous.

I sent her soothing thoughts, but we didn't talk much. There were other players needing attention.

Carrel squeezed my hand and stood up.

"Well, Harvey," she said, clearing her throat. "I have to go play now."

I caught her hand and pulled her back.

"Carrell," I said. "You don't *have* to go play. You *get* to go play. There's a world of difference."

A sudden grin lit the worry off her face.

"You're right," she said. "What am I scared of? This is fun!"

I wish I could say Carrell won the tournament. For sure I can report that she received great pleasure from playing in it. Never again have I heard her say she *has* to play golf.

Playing golf is a privilege, not a sentence.

Flavor That Lasts

IF YOU WERE asked to imagine what flavor of ice cream would describe your golf swing, I would like to hear you answer, "vanilla."

The more simple your approach to the swing is, the better off you are. It's the simple things that last.

The Oracle Speaks

HARRIS GREENWOOD, A college player of mine who later became a lawyer in Houston, filled me in on the background of this story long after it happened.

The way Harris told it, there was a young golfer in his Houston crowd who was their equal or better in daily games. This fellow would win money from them, but in the weekend tournaments, his scores were inexplicably high. Rather than winning the weekend tournaments, as this fellow had the talent to do, he finished in the middle of the pack.

Harris had always come to me for lessons, as had several others in that Houston bunch. They started telling this fellow, "Harvey can solve all your problems. If you can just spend a little time with Harvey, he will heal you. Harvey will touch your clubs and give you his blessing, and all will be okay."

I didn't know this was going on, of course. When Harris phoned me to arrange a lesson for this fellow, he just told me his friend needed help.

He scheduled the lesson for five weeks in advance. Harris and his friends wanted the time to continue fooling with this fellow's mind. They counted down the days. They told him, "Harvey is the high priest of golf. He will do magic. The rest of us will never be in the winner's circle again. You will become a dominant force in amateur golf after you visit Harvey."

The night before the lesson, this fellow drove to Austin. He spent the night at the Terrace Motel and went to bed early.

Now I enter the story.

It is barely daylight, and I am in the golf shop at Austin Country Club. This young fellow comes in and introduces himself as my pupil from Houston. I tell him to take a couple of buckets of balls and go warm up.

Later I wander out to the practice tee and watch him. I am surprised. This fellow hits it like a pro. I don't say a word. I rest my chin in my hand and stand behind him, stand at every angle, watching in admiration as this fellow hits shot after shot as crisply as you please.

For a whole hour this fellow hits balls. I don't say a word except to tell him when to switch to a different club.

At last it is time for me to say something.

I can tell by the anxious way he bites his lip that he is expecting to hear a decree from an oracle.

"Well, son," I say. "You line up to the ball real well. You have a good strong grip that I like. You stay down and behind the ball well. You hit it solid. Would you mind telling me what were your last two scores?"

"I played in a tournament last weekend," he says. "I shot a 77 on Saturday and would have had about 78 on Sunday, except I put the ball in my pocket."

"There's only one thing I see wrong with your game," I say.

"What is it?" he cries.

"Your scores are too high," I say.

This fellow is speechless. Then he becomes irate.

"Is that all?" he says.

"That's all I can see."

He takes his clubs over to his car, slams the trunk shut, slams the driver's door, and roars off on his way back to Houston.

Now I leave the story again, so far as I know.

Back in Houston—Harris told me later—this fellow at first wouldn't tell them about his lesson. They kept pushing him for details. They pushed until he blew up. "That Harvey Penick is a fraud!" he yelled. "He doesn't know anything about golf! He didn't give me a single bit of instruction that will help my swing! He just told me I ought to shoot better scores! I didn't need to drive all the way to Austin to have some old fool tell me my scores are too high!"

The next weekend this young fellow went out and won his first golf tournament.

Apparently all he needed was to be told it was all right for him to do it.

A Story by Helen

THE TELEPHONE RINGS frequently in the kitchen of our home near Austin Country Club.

Unless one of Harvey's day nurses get the phone while I'm shopping or playing cards—I love bridge and gin rummy—I'm the one who answers.

Harvey sits in his favorite chair in the living room beyond the open kitchen door. He is about twenty feet from the phone. But Harvey hasn't been able to walk for several years now, and his hearing is poor. It is a terrible strain for him to try to talk on the phone.

As a result, I have become the translator between Harvey and his callers.

You can't believe some of the calls I have answered.

I have given putting lessons to golf pros on the phone, shouting their questions to Harvey.

All sorts of people phone Harvey, from golf pros to average players to fans and friends and those who are just plain curious.

Recently I picked up the phone and heard a man say, "Put Harvey Penick on the line, please."

I explained about Harvey's problem with the phone.

"Well, you tell him I am coming to see him for a week of lessons," the man said.

"I don't know if Harvey will be able to see you," I said. "Especially not for a whole week. It's a bit too hard on him."

"What's hard about it?"

I said, "Harvey is getting along in years, you know."

"He is, is he?" the man said. "You tell him to fire up and get ready to teach. I'm leaving in a few minutes, driving down there from Sacramento."

I said, "I'm afraid you are wasting your time."

The man said, "Nope, I have no time to waste. You see, I am ninety years old myself."

I'm sure Harvey will see him, but the man hasn't arrived. I hope his time didn't run out while he was on his way.

Another Call

I HEARD THE PHONE RING, and moments later Helen appeared in the kitchen doorway.

"Harvey, this is a woman calling from Providence, Rhode Island. Her name is Paula Granoff. She says she has played golf for years but had never won anything until she read your *Little Red Book*. Right after she read it, she won the Rhode Island Senior Amateur."

"Tell her, congratulations on her good playing," I said.

Helen spoke on the phone again. Then she returned to the door.

"She wants to come to Austin and take lessons," Helen said.

"If she just won the state championship, what does she need with lessons?" I said.

After another phone conversation, Helen came all the way into the living room and stood beside my chair.

"Harvey, she says she wants to come to Texas to meet the great teacher," Helen said. "I wonder who on earth she has in mind?"

Toss It

ONE AFTERNOON, I was standing at the edge of the putting green with Ben Crenshaw and his good friend Billy Munn, who had been captain of one of my university golf teams and my number-one player.

Billy had talked to me about turning pro when his college career ended. But this was in the early sixties. Billy's hometown, Midland, was rich with oil money, and the pro golf tour paid off in peanuts, compared to the winning purses of today. A young man of means in Midland in Billy's day was expected to take up a career as a banker, doctor, lawyer, or oil man—not as a golf pro.

He had asked me what he should do. This was Billy's whole life we were talking about. I certainly didn't want to tell him the wrong thing. All I said to him was, "Billy, whichever career you choose will not give you integrity. You have to bring integrity with you."

Billy chose the oil business—partly because he'd had four knee operations and wasn't sure he could stand up to the physical grind of the tour.

This day, on the edge of the putting green with Billy and Ben, we were discussing what club to use to chip the ball to a hole near the outside of the green.

"Ben, you're a good athlete," I said. "Pick up a ball and toss it underhand close to that hole."

The ball rolled to within a foot of the cup.

"You tossed that ball real low," I said. "Why didn't you throw it high up in the air, like it would have gone if you had been using an open-face wedge?"

"Because you said to get it close," Ben said.

"Exactly," I said. "What club would produce the same flight and result of that underhand toss you just made? Whatever club you think would do it, that's the club to choose."

An Irony

IN GOLF YOUR strengths and weaknesses will always be there. If you could improve your weaknesses, you would improve your game.

The irony is that people prefer to practice their strengths.

The First Choice

WHEN YOU ARE TRYING to decide which club to hit, the first one that comes to mind is the right one.

Let us suppose your instinct tells you to pull a 5-iron out of the bag.

Your instinct is correct. Hit the 5-iron.

But you throw up some grass to test the wind and you check the yardage again, and you overrule your instinct. You change to a 4-iron, or maybe to a 6-iron.

Now you are no longer sure. You'll probably ease up on the 4-iron or really bear down on the 6-iron. The result is liable to be a poor shot.

Go ahead and hit the club your inner voice first tells you to hit. If your judgment is a little off, so what? It's only a few yards' difference between clubs.

The important difference is in confidence.

Confidence is contagious.

A Strange World

CALL ME OLD-FASHIONED or starchy or whatever you will, but two things in this world I just can't grow accustomed to are a man and a woman living together without being married—and taking a mulligan at golf.

Look Here First

NINE OUT OF TEN problems with the swing of the average golfer begin with the grip or the stance.

The symptoms that come from these two sources are many and various.

It is easy for teachers to get caught up in treating the symptoms without first going to the underlying causes in the grip and the stance.

Toward a Stronger Grip

FOR A NUMBER of years during Ben Hogan's prime and thereafter, many golf teachers taught the neutral grip—in which the V's of the thumbs and forefingers point more or less toward the nose or right eye.

This was Hogan's grip, and it was the right thing for him because he was always fighting a hook. In fact, most good players tend to be hookers. This neutral grip worked well for the good players and still does.

For players who are not so good, the neutral grip encourages a slice.

Recently, some gentlemen from Tokyo came to visit with me at Austin Country Club. We were sitting in the grassy patio, nibbling at hors d'ouevres from a tray, drinking iced tea, and chatting about golf through an interpreter.

Mr. Tsuyoshi Honjo, editor in chief of *Baffy* magazine, asked if I would look at his grip. He removed his jacket, rolled up his sleeves, and placed his hands on a 7-iron that was sent out from the golf shop.

His V's pointed straight at his nose.

"I see you have read Ben Hogan's book," I said.

"Oh yes, oh yes," he beamed. "Everyone has read Mr. Hogan's book."

"I imagine you are quite a slicer," I said.

"Oh yes, oh yes," he said, not so happily. "Very big slice."

I asked him to roll both his hands to the right until his V's pointed at his right shoulder. I tossed a little tiny carrot off the tray, into the grass at his feet.

"Hit that carrot," I said.

We kept it up for half an hour, Mr. Tsuyoshi Honjo hitting tiny carrots off the patio grass with a 7-iron and a strong grip.

The reason I wanted him to hit the carrots instead of golf balls is that he would have no expectation about hitting carrots, and so his mind would be free to concentrate on the grip and the swing. If we had put a golf ball in front of him, he would probably get tense. (Later I told Tommy Kite about this. He grinned and said, "You have a new saying now—clip the carrot.")

"How does that grip feel?" I asked my Japanese visitor.

"I think I hit it much harder and farther." He smiled.

"Please practice that grip and that swing, hitting carrots or leaves or twigs, until you feel good about it," I said. "Then go to the practice range and use the grip and swing on some golf balls. I think you will be pleased."

The Japanese gentlemen were quite excited when they left the patio on their way to pay a call on Columbia Lakes, near Houston, where Kathy Whitworth, Betsy Cullen, and Mark Steinbauer are teaching.

In the last few years I have noticed that the golf grip is evolving back toward a stronger position. In the days of Vardon, the V's pointed at the right shoulder. During the era of Hogan, the V's moved to point at the nose. Now, in the days of Freddie Couples, Davis Love III, John Daly, and others, the grip has once again moved the V's toward the right shoulder.

I believe this is because of all the good modern players who have learned to combine the hands-and-arms swing of the strong grip with the big muscle swing of the neutral grip.

Without a doubt, the strong grip is better for the average player. As Mr. Tsuyoshi Honjo said, a less-than-expert player soon feels he can hit the ball harder and farther with a strong grip.

But like any other golf teaching, a strong grip can be overdone.

Kathy, Betsy, and Mark teach, among others, groups of young Japanese women who are selected to come to Columbia Lakes to train to be golf professionals.

They brought some of their Japanese pupils to see me at the practice area at Austin Country Club. The girls were each told to hit a few 5-irons for me. One girl in particular really gave that ball a smack.

"What do you think of her?" Kathy said.

"I think she can't hit a driver," I said.

The young Japanese understood me. She smiled and pulled out of her pocket a tee four inches long. That's how high she had to tee it up to use her driver.

It was all in her grip. This girl's grip was four-knuckles, V's pointed to the right of the right shoulder, like an old West-Texas grip. With that grip, she de-lofted the club so much that it took a four-inch tee for her driver to reach the ball.

"Let me see your golf club," I said.

The Japanese girl ducked her head bashfully and handed me the club. As I had suspected, it was not a 5-iron. It was a 7-iron. Her grip was turning it into a 4-iron.

She had learned that grip at home, I must point out—not at Columbia Lakes.

All You Need to Know About the Wrist Cock

So MUCH HAS BEEN WRITTEN and spoken about it that the wrist cock has become a literature of its own.

Let's keep it simple.

Take your stance. Swing your club back to waist high. If the toe of your club is pointing straight up, the wrist cock is built into your swing. Think no more about it.

To see the wrist cock in your living room without a

golf club, just take your stance. Let your left arm hang down and put your right arm behind your back to get it out of the way.

Make your left hand like a blade, the back of the hand facing your imaginary target down the line. Swing your left arm back to the top of your backswing and stop.

Clench your left hand into a fist.

Your wrist is cocked. Now you know how it feels.

Another way to get the feeling of a cocked wrist is to swing your left fist all the way through as if it were holding a golf club.

That's all you need. I would prefer that you delve no further into the literature of the wrist cock.

Higher Aspects

PEOPLE SAY TO ME that golf is a *spiritual* game. I don't believe I understand how that word applies to golf. According to my dictionary, the first meaning of *spiritual* is "Of the spirit or the soul as distinguished from the body."

It is true that golf is a game in which you seem to get in touch with higher parts of yourself. We can say golf is spiritual in that respect. But we can't leave the body out of the golf swing, can we?

All my life I have been asking people what the difference is between faith and confidence.

One of my pupils told me, "Confidence is that feeling I get just before I learn better."

Another said, "Confidence in golf is when I am faced with a certain shot that I have hit successfully many times, and I know full well I will do it again. Faith is when I may never have hit this particular shot before, but I trust that I can do it because I have faith in my swing."

Most people say faith is religious, but they feel that confidence is something different.

My dictionary says faith is "Unquestioning belief in God, religion, or a system of religious beliefs."

Confidence, according to my dictionary, is "Firm belief in the truth or reality of a fact, or trust and reliance on one's own abilities."

It seems to me that confidence is the feeling we want to have in playing golf. But we can't dismiss the value of faith, either.

I think faith is in the heart, and confidence is in the mind.

A Method for
Madness

A FRIEND WROTE me a letter from Sawgrass Country Club in Ponte Vedra, Florida.

He wanted to know, "How can I keep from getting so insanely mad on the golf course? I know losing my temper is not good for my game. But when I blow a short putt and then hook a drive into the marsh, I go crazy with anger and despair. Then things get rapidly worse. I know it's stupid to get mad but what can I do?"

I think it is fine to get mad if you hit a poor shot or miss a putt you should have made. Getting mad shows you have the competitive spirit. They call him "Gentle Ben" Crenshaw, but he's always had flashes of temper on the course because he wants to win and he wants to be the best.

So get mad. But do it in a gentlemanly way.

In your mind call yourself every name you can think of for the poor shot you just hit.

But while you are being mad, be mad only at yourself.

Do not be mad at your clubs or the golf course. They're the same as they were when you hit a great shot yesterday. And don't be mad at luck. Stick to the one thing you can control: you.

Then forget it. Cast the bad names out of your mind and be thinking positively by the time you approach your next shot. Your next shot is a new experience. It might be the best shot you ever hit in your life.

Making a Comeback

EVERY TEACHER IS familiar with this pupil.

He is about fifty years old. He was a good player as a youth and was a long hitter off the tee. A person's memory tends to add a good many yards to his youthful tee shots. But this pupil I am describing really was a long hitter and had some success in amateur tournaments.

After college he went into a business or a profession and did well at it. He kept playing golf through his twenties. Gradually he began to play only on weekends. The demands of family and his striving to be good at his chosen calling eventually left him with no time for golf.

At about age thirty he was playing maybe three or four times a year at charity events or conventions. His scores climbed into the 90s. He was embarrassed to play poorly. He remembered what a joy the game had been when he was near scratch. Those days, he decided, were gone forever.

He packed his clubs in the closet and gave it up.

Twenty years later, his kids have left the nest, his wife is busy with volunteer work, his finances look pretty comfortable, and he finds he has increasing free time. His thoughts drift back to golf.

He arranges for a lesson.

The first morning on the practice range, after we get to know each other a little, I ask why he has driven all the way from Dallas to take a lesson from me at Austin Country Club.

He admits he had a lesson from another teacher the previous week, but he wasn't satisfied. He starts to show me what the other teacher had told him.

"If you don't mind," I say, cutting him off politely, "I had rather not hear what someone else told you. Please hit a few balls with your 7-iron, and I will watch."

He says, "Pro, my big problem is my loss of distance. I've been hitting balls on my own for a couple of months. I get worse and worse. The more balls I hit, the shorter they go. I don't understand it. I lift weights, I use hand-grippers daily, and I jog three miles every morning. I'm in the best shape I've been in since I was twenty-five years old. And yet I've lost all my distance."

His mention of lifting weights is a red flag.

I strongly believe in physical conditioning. In my opinion, the main reason the modern touring pros hit the ball so far is that they are stronger and in better shape than the pros of early days. But a golfer must be extremely careful about weight lifting. He may strengthen the wrong muscles and hurt his swing instead of helping it.

"Let's leave distance for later," I tell this pupil. "See

that flag near that small stone wall about 150 yards down there? Hit a ball to that flag for me."

He hits several shots. I don't watch the ball. I watch his swing.

"You are aiming west and trying to hit north," I tell him.

"I'm aiming a little to the left so I can hit out on the ball," he says.

"Lee Trevino can aim west and hit north, because he lets his head drop down half a foot as he hits the ball. I want you to stand up taller and aim square to the hole. Or even aim a little to the right of the hole and play a right-to-left shot."

I back up my golf cart and turn it to point straight at the flag. I ask him to square up his stance to my cart and hit balls directly at the target.

He makes a few more swings. I stop him.

"I'm going to tell you something you are not going to like," I say. "If you are not going to follow my advice, we are both wasting our time. You're like most Dallas people—always in a hurry. Dallas people do everything like they are working by the job. I want you to work by the hour."

He swiftly rakes over another ball to hit, but I stop him again.

"I'm not going to tell you a negative thing, like not to swing so hard, and I'm not going to tell you to swing slow," I say. "Just swing like you're doing it by the hour. There's no rush."

I ask him to put the ball on a low tee.

"Now," I say. "Work by the hour and cut off that tee, and I will show you a good shot."

Swing after swing, over and over, I repeat the instructions.

"You know," I say at last, "sitting here telling you the same thing over and over again doesn't make either of us look very bright. If you want your distance back, you'll do it by hitting the ball solid, not by hitting it fast. You're going to have to learn to work by the hour and cut off the tee to get your distance back."

The magical word "distance" persuades him to try to do as I ask. He hits a few good ones. He grins. He hits a bad one. I notice he changes his grip.

"Don't worry about making an adjustment every time you hit a bad shot," I say. "Never make a change based on one shot, or even a few shots. Wait for a pattern to develop."

He says he has taken up wearing glasses since his glorious youth, and perhaps he does not see the ball so well.

I tell him Jimmy Demaret used to throw down three or four balls on the tee during a practice round and hit each of them perfectly while looking at the gallery and telling jokes.

"If your swing is grooved, you can hit the ball with a sack over your head," I say. "Let's keep on clipping off that tee and working by the hour."

At last he understands that I have told him all I am going to tell him by way of instruction in this lesson, and if he doesn't clip off the tee and work by the hour, it has been a fruitless trip from Dallas.

When the realization sinks in, he begins hitting the ball solidly. I put a 3-wood in his hands. He hits the ball far and with a right-to-left tail on it.

He is thrilled. My arms tingle with pleasure.

"One more thing," I say as the lesson is ending. "Promise me you won't reach for your driver until you are able to hit the fairway ten times out of ten with your 3-wood."

"Thanks, Pro," he says. "I'll keep practicing, and maybe I'll try to qualify for the National Amateur next summer. Do you think I have a chance?"

"Sure you have a chance," I say. "If you can putt."

A Distinction

THE ABILITY to concentrate is good, but thinking too much about how you are doing what you are doing is disastrous.

Trust your muscles and hit the ball to the hole. Keep it simple.

Preacher Mann

THE FIRST TIME Dr. Gerald Mann, pastor of the River-bend Baptist Church, came to me for a golf lesson, we started in the customary way with him hitting a 7-iron and trying to clip off the tee.

He hit a hook and I said, "I don't believe it. Hit another."

Again he hit a hook. I asked him to hit several more balls, and all were hooks.

He said, "Why are you looking at me like that?"

"I still don't believe what I am seeing, and I thought I had seen every kind of golf swing there is. Everything about your grip, address, and swing tells me you should be shanking the ball. But you're hooking it. You have a God-given athletic ability."

We ended that first lesson on the positive thought that Dr. Mann was blessed with athletic ability. It was a long while before he came back to let me help him with the fundamentals.

I have played a lot of golf with preachers. One minister I recall would, after missing a short putt, turn to another member of the group and ask, "Would you mind expressing aloud my sentiments about that?"

As anyone who has played with him will tell you, Gerald Mann is not at all reluctant to express his sentiments.

Tom and Christy Kite and their kids attend the Riverbend Baptist Church.

On the Sunday in the summer of 1992 when Tommy was about to tee off for the final round of the U.S. Open at Pebble Beach, Dr. Mann told his congregation:

"I don't know if God is into golf. But I am praying for Tom Kite to win the Open, and I want you to pray for him, too. If you don't want to pray for Tommy, I suggest you go someplace where they don't pray for winners."

The Reason for It

I HAVE ALWAYS TRIED to impress on my members and my pupils that the rules of golf are made to protect you, not for you to gain by them.

From the Fringe

ON A PAR FOUR, if your ball is on the fringe of the green in two strokes and you require three more strokes to get into the hole, you might as well have whiffed your tee shot.

The penalty is the same—the loss of one stroke.

If you whiffed your tee shot, you would be embarrassed. But if you take three from the fringe, you are apt to say, "Well, that's just my game."

You should feel that you can get down in two from the fringe every time. Practice it. There's no use throwing away all those strokes.

South of the Border

GOLF TEACHER CHUCK COOK tells the story that shortly after World War II a promising young player in Los Angeles asked noted amateur Wilford Wehrle for a lesson.

Wehrle broke open a sleeve of brand-new Spalding

balls and tossed one onto the ground at the youngster's feet.

"Let's see you hit it," Wehrle said.

Already nervous to be in Wehrle's company, the young player now was thoroughly frightened. He had never even seen a brand-new golf ball before. During the war, new golf balls scarcely ever entered a civilian's hands.

The youngster made a swing, caught the ball thin, and cut a horrible gash in it.

Wehrle muttered an oath and tossed another new Spalding onto the grass.

"Try it again," he said.

The trembling youngster topped the ball and nearly cut it in half.

Disgusted, Wehrle grabbed the iron club out of the youngster's hand and began swinging it into the ground, tearing up big chunks of earth.

In his anger Wehrle chopped a dozen huge divots.

"Son," he yelled, "the first thing you've got to learn is that golf is a game of digging holes!"

It is, of course, true that one of the paradoxes of golf is that you must hit down on the ball to make it rise.

A most common fault with beginners—and with poor players who have struggled for years—is trying to help the ball into the air by hitting it on the upswing with an iron club.

Until you learn to hit down and through the ball, you cannot play a decent iron shot.

However, I am not a believer in digging big divots. I believe it is better to pick the ball off the grass than to hoe it.

There are great players, I know, who whack out divots

the size of pie pans. But what I like to see is a shallow divot that is shaped like a dollar bill, the sort of divot Byron Nelson produced.

This reminds me of a teaching job I had at the Club Compestre in Monterrey, Mexico.

The person who hired me said, "Harvey, can you spare a couple of weeks to come give lessons at our club? We really need help."

"What is the problem?" I asked.

He said, "Our whole club is full of shankers."

In the autumn, I flew down to Monterrey. Sure enough, it was a club full of shankers. I hate to use that word—a "lateral shot" sounds nicer—because it conjures up one of the ugliest sights in golf.

But there was no getting around it.

This club was infested with shankers, as if they all had a disease.

It didn't take me long to discover the reason.

The club's regular teaching pro—who was away on vacation—had one firm principle that he drummed into his pupils. He told them, "Hit down, hit down, hit down, and hit down!"

Golf, for him, was truly a game of digging holes.

The danger in hitting down on the ball with such intensity is that you are likely to shank it.

If you are going to play golf by digging holes, you must have a good, fast hip turn and hit through the ball, or you can expect to foul it into the dugout.

I spent a couple of pleasant weeks in the brisk mountain climate of Monterrey, teaching the club members that there is more to golf than digging holes.

I believe it is impossible to shank a ball with a closed

blade. It was a joy to see their happiness when their shank went away.

When it was time for me to return to Austin, they paid me off in cash—a fat roll of big, very colorful bills.

I had never seen that much money. I don't remember now how much it translated to back in Texas, but it made me about half nervous to have so much cash. I stretched rubber bands around the roll and then tied a piece of string around it, stuffed the money into my pocket and tied the string to my belt loop.

Sitting on the plane, waiting to take off, the fellow next to me leaned over and said, "Excuse me. Isn't your name Harvey?"

I said yes.

He said, "They're paging you. They want you back inside the airport."

I thought, oh my gosh, they've come to their senses and realized they paid me way too much. I'm going to have to march right in there and give this big roll of money back to them.

But that wasn't it at all. It was just some minor thing with the luggage. I got back home with the whole roll.

And you know what? The next autumn, they hired me to come back to the same club for another two weeks of teaching.

Their regular pro had returned after I left, and started drilling them again to hit down, hit down, and hit down.

They all started shanking again.

The Lay Up

ONE OF THE WORST SHOTS in golf is when a player decides to lay up short of a hazard and yet hits enough club to reach the trouble—and usually does.

Often this is because the player chooses a club that will land close as possible short of the hazard. He hits it easy, he thinks. But his easy swing catches the ball solid and it goes ten yards farther than usual.

If you are laying up, be sure you lay up and not in.

You might think of the shot as "laying back" from the hazard, rather than "laying up" to the edge of it.

Tommy Wins the Open

ON THE FINAL DAY of the 1992 U.S. Open at Pebble Beach, with the wind and rain howling in off the ocean, Tommy Kite played one of the finest, most courageous rounds of golf in the history of the game.

Sitting in front of my television back home in Austin,

I was so moved and so proud of Tommy that my toes curled up and I cried like a baby when they put the championship trophy in his hands at the end of that excruciating day.

When Tommy came by to visit with me sometime later, I asked what he had been thinking about during the hours he was battling horrible weather conditions to emerge as champion over the best players in the world.

I have always impressed on my pupils that when they're playing in the wind and rain and cold, they should take their time. I don't mean play slow. I mean just don't hurry.

So it warmed my heart when Tommy said, "I was thinking, 'Take your time.' "

I asked him to tell me about it.

"In a situation like that," he said, "with players being blown away, somehow you've got to forget about your swing or any mechanical thoughts and get into a really trusting mentality.

"You just have to take the attitude that you have done all the training that is required, and if you're not going to trust it, why do all the training?"

He got that line from sports psychologist Dr. Bob Rotella. I love that line. Trust it.

"I use that thought an awful lot when I'm on the golf course and have a chance to win the tournament," Tommy said. "I keep telling myself to trust it, just go ahead and trust it.

"There's no point in training and working hard if when you get out there on the golf course or the football field or whatever, you're not going to trust the fact that you know how to do it. Like Troy Aikman. He trusts himself to throw the football where he wants to put it. Otherwise, why should he bother with all that practice?

"As for taking my time, I mean I want to be totally ready to play the shot before I play the shot. I must be 100 percent committed to playing this particular shot at this particular moment. In bad weather, if it takes a little longer to get ready, then I need to take a little longer."

We remembered one year at the Masters when Ben Crenshaw was preparing to hit his approach shot to the 72nd hole. Ben needed a birdie to win his second Masters or a par to get into a playoff. It was raining. Ben's glove was wet. He missed the green, made a bogey on the hole, and finished second.

"Ben just got into a little bit of a rush," Tommy said. "It would only have taken a minute for him to reach in his bag and pull out a brand-new dry glove right out of a package and feel good about it.

"It was kind of like he was thinking, well, you know, it's okay, I can hit this shot anyway. And then when you miss it, you're kicking yourself in the rear all the way.

"Lee Trevino made the comment, 'I don't care if you have to send your caddie into the pro shop to buy a new glove. When you've got the Masters laying on the line, you don't hit the ball until you are ready.' I'm not picking on Ben when I say this, because I've done dumb things like that way too often.

"When I woke up Sunday morning at the Open and stepped outside and felt the wind and rain in my face, I knew I had an excellent chance to win if I just took my time and trusted myself."

Tommy took dead aim that day.

A Story by
Christy Kite

AFTER TOM WON THE Open on Sunday, he was supposed to play an outing in St. Louis the next day. Monterey, California, is not the easiest place in the world to get out of, so I decided I would fly to St. Louis with him and then fly home to Austin on Monday morning rather than spending the night by myself in Monterey.

They had two private planes waiting to take us to St. Louis. Most people took the earlier one. The only people on the later plane were Craig Stadler and us.

The plane was delayed, so Craig went to dinner. We were waiting for him to come back. Now it was just Tom and I on the plane, and we had the U.S. Open Trophy with us.

Tom said, "You'll be flying home tomorrow, but the first thing Tuesday morning, I want you to take this trophy over to Mr. Penick and set it right in his lap."

Tuesday morning, I took the trophy to Austin Country Club, where Mr. Penick was giving a lesson to a woman who had come down from Rhode Island to see him.

I walked up to his golf cart and said, "Mr. Penick, this is for you."

I put the U.S. Open Trophy in his lap.

I said, "Tom said a big piece of this trophy belongs to you."

Mr. Penick started crying. I started crying. Pretty soon all the people around his cart were crying and laughing at the same time.

I wish Tom could have been there to give Mr. Penick the trophy himself, but he couldn't, and I did it the way Tom wanted me to do it. It was a great pleasure, that's for sure.

Make Up Your Mind

ON EVERY KIND of golf shot, you must make up your mind exactly what it is you want to do. Do not have the slightest doubt. As a friend of mine says of the way he lives his life, "I may be wrong, but I am never in doubt."

If there is doubt in your mind over a golf shot, how can your muscles know what they are expected to do?

What most average players can't seem to grasp is that this is just as true of a two-foot putt as it is of any other shot.

Watching the Bob Hope Tournament on television one Saturday, I saw Tommy Kite coming down the stretch miss a putt that was so short, he could easily have kicked it in.

The television commentator said Tommy's stroke

broke down. Well, I could see that it wasn't a great stroke, but I doubted if mechanics had anything to do with missing the putt.

On Sunday, Tommy holed everything he looked at, shot a course record, and won the tournament going away at 35 under par.

When he came home, I asked him about that putt he missed on Saturday.

"I'd had the same putt in a practice round," he said. "The green back there has so much slope to it that it looks like it breaks off the world. When I stood over the putt in the tournament, I was thinking it was just outside the right edge of the hole. But I looked again and thought, whoa, I'm playing too much break. I know it breaks a lot, but, gosh, does it break this much?

"Instead of stepping back and starting over with a clear mind, I stroked the putt and missed it. Missing the putt had nothing to do with the stroke. I missed it because I wasn't thinking right. I wasn't ready to play the shot.

"Sunday I knew I was going to putt well. All I did was make up my mind I would be totally committed to every stroke."

If this is what is required of the U.S. Open champion, how can the average golfer expect to get by with less?

The California
Woman

I WAS GIVING a lesson to a woman from California who already had a pretty good game, but wanted to lower her handicap to a single number.

Something was wrong.

She was hitting the ball decently, but she kept frowning and fidgeting.

After half an hour she said, "Harvey, what you are telling me is too simple. It is so simple that I can't understand it."

It wasn't the first time I have been criticized for being too simple, nor was it the last.

Some pupils are not happy unless the teacher gives them plenty of technical talk to chew on. They want the teacher to fill their minds with "golf-swing theory."

These pupils leave me and move on to other, smarter teachers.

No hard feelings on my part.

From my point of view, I don't teach theory. I teach simple things that produce good results.

The woman from California said, "I don't understand what you mean by 'clip off the tee.' "

"But you've been doing it," I said. "Are you unhappy with the results?"

"No, the results are fine. What I want to know is *why* the results are fine."

"Because when you clip off the tee you square your clubface," I said.

"I know that," she said. "But *why* does it square my clubface?"

"It's natural," I said.

"That's not a good enough answer," she said.

A few days earlier, the touring pro Tommy Aaron had come to the club for a lesson. I watched him hit balls all afternoon. At the end he said, "Well, what's the answer?"

I said, "You hit the ball beautifully. Ball-striking is not the reason you aren't winning."

"So what is the reason?" he asked.

"I don't know," I said.

That was not the answer Tommy wanted, but it was honest.

The woman from California stuck her club back in the bag, peeled off her glove, and said, "You make it sound too easy. My husband is the one you ought to be teaching. He's dumb enough to understand you. What do I owe you for this lesson?"

"Nothing," I said.

"You can't mean that."

"How could I charge you money for not helping you?" I said.

"But this is embarrassing. I must pay you for your time."

She left angry that I wouldn't take her money. There's no pleasing some people.

The Judge

HE WAS A JUDGE from out of town.

His overlapping stomach presented the judge with a dilemma. If he stood where he could see the ball, he couldn't reach it. If he stood where he could hit the ball, he couldn't see it.

After five lessons in a week, I had done very little to improve the judge's golf swing. But he was preparing to return home, and I wanted to give him at least one positive thought.

"Judge," I said, "I have a suggestion that will help make your game more fun."

"What is it?" he asked.

"Always play with clean golf balls."

Keep It Moving

POOR PLAYERS USUALLY seem embarrassed to play with good players.

The fact is that you may not be good enough to play with the good players, but no one will notice if you keep up.

The good players are not going to be watching you and criticizing your swing. They have their own games to deal with.

But if you hold up play, the others will notice you—and probably not in a kindly manner.

If you, as a poor player, lose your temper along with your golf balls, and shout and throw clubs and curse your luck, and plumb-bob all your putts from both sides of the hole, the good players will be disgusted. They'll avoid you for the rest of your life, not only on the golf course, but in the social and business worlds as well.

So just keep the game moving in a good humor, and you will always be welcome.

The Learning Game

A WOMAN FROM BOSTON wrote a letter asking if I would help her husband with his putting.

Her husband, she said, is a senior and a good player. His usual score is about 75. But lately his putting has gone sour. So sour, in fact, that it was making him hard to live with.

"Could he come to Austin and take a couple of lessons from you to straighten out his stroke?" she wrote.

In my opinion, I told her, the best thing her husband could do would be to stay right there in Boston and take up playing a little game that will cure what ails him.

If he's a senior who shoots 75, her husband already has a good putting stroke. Most likely what is wrong with his putting is not his stroke, but his touch.

This is what I suggested:

Her husband should take his putter and one ball and go round and round and round the putting green. Be sure to putt the ball into the cup on every hole.

I said her husband should gather a few of his senior friends who have the time and start a daily putting game. Play for a dime a hole—not enough money to make anyone nervous, but enough to keep score.

After a few weeks of this, her husband will be putting better than ever before in his life. And so will his friends.

I can't say this too often. You seniors—or Seasoned Citizens—grab your putter and one ball and head for that practice green.

Maybe you no longer hit the ball as far as the younger players. But there's not a reason in the world why you can't out-putt them.

A Story by Tom Kite

THERE WAS A TIME when I was probably fifteen or sixteen years old and had been working with Mr. Penick for about four years, and I had some success at one of those junior tournaments. I came back sort of full of myself.

Somehow I guess the word filtered back to Mr. Penick that I had gotten a little cocky.

(For thirty years he has been telling me to call him Harvey, but I just can't do it. It may be the only instruction he has ever given me that I can't follow. My respect for him is so deep that I may try to say "Harvey," but it comes out "Mr. Penick.")

Anyway, fresh from my junior triumph, I asked him to give me a lesson.

We went to the practice range, and he watched me hit some shots. We did the things we normally do.

As we finished, he started to walk away, and then he turned to me and said, "Tommy, you've been having a lot of success. You have been playing really well, and I am very proud of you. But I want you to remember this: You are what you are, not what you do."

Then he walked off.

Oh, man. It was like hitting me with a ton of bricks. It was like taking a two-by-four and slapping me up the side of my head.

There was no doubt in my mind what he meant.

I have tried to live by that statement ever since.

The True Way

I WAS WATCHING four of my University of Texas players getting ready to hit on the first tee one afternoon in the early spring.

They were discussing whether to play "winter" rules or "summer" rules.

"What do you think, Coach?"

I said, "Well, you boys can go play golf. Or else you can make up some other game and go play that, instead."

They understood my meaning.

In the game of golf, the ball is played as you find it.

Club Selection

GOOD PLAYERS AT ANY LEVEL share the skill of knowing what club to pull out of the bag.

I say "any level" because there are many high handicappers who are good players at their level. They always shoot their handicaps and can make a match against anyone.

But the average player doesn't know how far he hits an iron shot. He has a rough idea of how far it would go if he hit his best shot. He is still not at all sure of this distance, anyhow; he may know the yardage, but not the golfing distance.

He makes a guess and pulls a club. He acts confident. Then he remembers the saying that confidence is the feeling you have just before you learn better.

With an inner lack of belief, he gets off a shot that may actually turn out all right now and then.

Think of what an advantage the good player who knows exactly how far he hits an iron has. He trusts his swing to do what he wants.

I have been lucky to see great players who had genius in picking the right club—Ben Hogan and Betsy Rawls come to mind at once—but I had a student and player at the University of Texas who was better than all.

His name was Wesley Ellis. He had a God-given gift to put his hand on the right club every time.

His dog used to follow him around the course and sit quietly while he hit a shot. I'll always remember that picture in my mind. I guess the dog had confidence in him, too.

A Special Club

IF SOMEONE GIVES you a driver, it might be wise to ask yourself, Why?

I never knew of a player to give away a driver he could hit really well.

For most everyone, the driver is the most difficult club in the bag. I have seen Arnold Palmer bring drivers into the workshop half a dozen at a time and file and whittle and scrape in an effort to get a club that felt just right to him. The next day he might be back with half a dozen more. When a player finds a driver he falls in love with, he keeps it forever—or at least until he falls out of love and divorces the club and sends it to live with eight or ten other drivers in the closet or the trunk of the car.

People are even stranger about their drivers than about their putters, as a rule.

I remember how in about 1962 a manufacturer came out with a new driver that had some kind of a slot in the head that supposedly increased distance. One of my

Texas boys, Billy Munn, told me he wanted to buy the new driver.

I said, "I didn't realize you had broken your old driver, Billy. Let's see if we can fix it."

There was nothing wrong with Billy's old driver, and he was good with it. Like all golfers, Billy was being gullible to the lure of advertising.

Byron Nelson tells a story that illustrates how players feel about their drivers.

In the middle 1930s, when he was a struggling young pro, Byron told his wife, Louise, that he needed to dig into their meager supply of money to buy a new driver.

Louise said, "Byron, since we've been married I haven't bought a new dress or a new pair of shoes, but in the past year you have bought four new drivers.

"Either you don't know what kind of driver you want, or else you don't know how to drive."

The next morning Byron took one of his drivers into the shop, working on it until it felt good in his hands, and played with it for a long time.

A Golfer's Prayer

DEAR GOD,
  In the annals of time
  a handful of citizens stood
  at the edge of a pasture.
With crooks in hand and stones about
  they made the first drives
  that one day would evolve into golf.

Just one of those first drivers had talent,
  and the rest were only determined.
That one talented driver drove the rest
  to lives of dedication, though often
  mediocrity and despair.

Grant us, O Lord, the grace to use the
  clubs you have blessed us with,
The disposition not to cloud
  our judgment and stance.

We beseech you, Lord, to heal our slice,
  to straighten our hook, to carve our
  divots truly, to improve our lie,
  making it just a tad better than our opponent's.

Give us the vision to keep our eye
  on the ball, our grip uncomfortable
  enough to be true, our minds and hearts
  pure as the course we play.

We ask this in Your Name.

  Amen.

> —Monsignor Richard E. McCabe
> at Caritas Charity Dinner
> Austin, Texas, November 24, 1992

Give Luck a Chance

DAVIS LOVE III had been playing on the tour for a while, and everyone could see he had a world of talent as well as a wonderful swing that he had been taught by his father, Davis, Jr., who was one of my University of Texas boys.

But Davis III had not won a tournament. So his dad brought him to me to see if I might have some idea that would help.

I watched Davis III hit some shots. He hit that ball like it was coming out of a cannon. It flew so fast and so far that I couldn't even follow it with my eyes.

But I could see well enough to follow his swing, of

course. I made a few small suggestions. Nothing much. Then we went to the practice green.

Davis III set up 15 feet from the hole and started stroking putts.

Oh my. Now I did see something I don't like.

Unless they hit the cup and rattled in, all those putts were going two or three feet past the hole.

I have always said that one of the worst sayings in golf is "Never up, never in."

Helen Dettweiler said that saying should be, "Always up, never in!"

Bobby Jones made the point that while a putt left short of the hole obviously didn't go in, neither did a putt that went past the hole. And there are many more three-putts coming back from beyond the cup than there are from just short of it.

After watching Davis III putt for a while, I said, "Son, I want you to try to get that ball to die somewhere around the hole. Work on your speed, your touch. Just roll the ball up there near the hole, and they'll start falling in. The idea is not to try to make every putt from this distance. You want to roll the ball to die at the hole."

I saw him thinking about it.

I said, "If you keep rolling the ball to die at the hole, you give luck a chance to happen."

A couple of weeks later, Davis III was on the 17th hole at Harbour Town with a 30-foot putt. He sank it and won the tournament.

His excited father phoned me that night.

Davis, Jr., said, "He told me, 'Dad, I did exactly what Mr. Penick was talking about. I rolled it up there and gave luck a chance to happen—and it did.' "

The Bench

A FELLOW DROVE down to Austin from somewhere in Ohio to take a lesson in chipping.

I visited with him for a while and repeated the first fundamental of the chipping stroke—make sure your hands stay ahead of, or even with, the clubhead all the way through.

Then I brought out a bench from the locker room and placed it on the edge of the green.

"Now I want you to chip the ball so that it goes under the bench and rolls to the hole," I said. "I'll be back around to see you in half an hour."

When I came back, he was chipping like an expert.

"That's it," I said. "Now you're a good chipper."

He hauled his clubs to his car and drove back to Ohio.

A couple of nights later, Helen answered the telephone at home.

"Harvey, this is some men calling from a club in Ohio," she said. "They say their friend has turned into a wonderful chipper, but he's also become a horrible liar. They don't believe all you did was tell him to chip under a bench."

A Teacher's Guide

In 1929, my sixth year as head pro, I pulled a pencil and a black ledger book out of a drawer in the golf shop and wrote for myself what could be called a guide to my thinking and behavior as a teacher and as a person.

I don't claim to be the creator of these principles. They are at least as old as the Bible. But I didn't write them in the black ledger book because I had learned them in Sunday school. I wrote them because I needed to use them in my everyday life.

This guide grew out of my experience as a caddie and shop manager and teacher. It is common sense. If it's so simple, why did I need to write it in the ledger in 1929?

In the midst of a lesson with a stubborn pupil that day, I found myself saying harshly, "I wish your brain and muscles were as coordinated as the clothes you're wearing!"

The look of hurt on the pupil's face caused me to apologize. I told him he was making progress and we would resume the lesson another day, by which time I would be a better teacher.

I walked into the golf shop, pulled out the ledger, and wrote the simple guide that I tried to follow for the rest of my life.

Like golf instruction, these principles are easy to learn, but useless unless they are put into action.

And like golf instruction, these principles are easy to forget. I need to read them every few days.

This is what I wrote:

○

Criticize yourself once in a while and see what you may be doing wrong. Never criticize others. It only stirs resentment. Speak no *ill* of anyone and *all* the good you know of everyone. Don't judge a person too soon. God waits until the end.

○

All people like to be important. Criticism from a teacher can kill the pupil's ambition to improve. Be anxious to praise and slow on fault-finding.

○

Nations and peoples also feel their importance. A top Eskimo feels superior to a Vanderbilt. Most people you meet feel superior to you in some way. Let them know you realize their importance, but avoid flattery.

○

Emerson said, "Everyone is my superior in some way." In that knowledge, I learn from them.

○

The best way to get pupils to do something is to get them to want to do it. Try to make the other person happy about doing something you suggest.

○

"Don't argue!" Even if you win, you usually lose your pupil's goodwill.

○

Don't tell pupils they are wrong. Most of us are prejudiced about ourselves. When we are wrong, we may admit it to ourselves—but not if someone is trying to force the "facts" down our throats.

○

I never know so much that I can't learn more.

○

Don't make direct contradictions to the sentiments of pupils combined with positive assertions of my own. Don't say, "Certainly, undoubtedly." Say, "I believe; I conceive; it appears at present; in some cases it might be right, but in the present case there seems to me some difference."

○

When I am at fault, simply say I am at fault and there is no excuse for it. I will do better next time, or at least I will change it.

○

Be friendly. Forget yourself. Stop thinking about "I." Listen to other people, keep interested in everyone else—caddies and members and all. Find out what they are doing and what they care about.

○

Try and remember names.

○

Try and talk plain.

○

A pro, or anyone, either goes forward or backward. What am I doing?

○

Try and be simple in living as well as in teaching or playing. The long odds are against us if we shoot the hard way.

○

Life consists of a lot of minor annoyances and few matters of real consequence.

○

We are frequently misjudged by our superiors, but never by our subordinates.

○

A stout heart usually accompanies a soft-spoken voice.

○

Finish one job well before starting another.

○

Listen to the kicks from anyone. You usually know the people and if they really have a kick coming.

○

Instead of doing what is right and best, we are influenced by associates. I must be an influence and example to members, caddies, and friends.

○

Always smile when you give anything, no matter how much it hurts. This means when giving service or anything else.

○

Be brave if you lose and meek if you win.

○

A good way to size up a person is to hear him say what he thinks it takes "guts" to do. A robber thinks it takes guts to do a daring job. A doctor thinks it takes guts to do a risky operation. A preacher probably believes it takes guts to tell his people to live according to the teachings of Jesus. The congregation will criticize him for it.

○

Teaching is a teacher's best advertisement. Caddies are good advertisers. They will watch you and copy you if they see that your teaching is good.

○

Practically all of the awkwardness and odd ways people have are an outgrowth of misunderstanding some of the few simple fundamentals.

o

I hear lots of shortcuts to par golf. But the only way to get there is with hard practice, sound style, and thought. I try to teach a pupil to swing the club correctly. The pupil must learn to hit the ball with that swing and get it in the hole.

o

Don't play too much golf or gamble at cards with the members. Call people *Mister* and *Mrs.* and make sure your assistants do the same. Stay away from the social angles of the club.

o

When I go to a doctor, all I ask is for him to have my interest at heart. I try to do that as a teacher. First of all, a teacher must try to understand what is going on in the pupil's mind. The teaching must be simple. Don't get technical. Put yourself in the pupil's place.

Musings on Rulings

MARK BROOKS, a University of Texas boy who now plays on the tour and is a member of Colonial Country Club in Fort Worth, stopped by to visit, and I was reminded of the time Mark was a victim of one of the silliest rules in golf.

I believe the rules of golf must be strictly obeyed. I believe the laws of the land should be obeyed, too, but that doesn't mean none of them should ever be changed.

Mark was getting ready to putt in a tournament. He marked his ball and rolled it across the green to his caddie to be cleaned. But the caddie missed the ball like a second baseman letting an easy grounder go between his legs. Mark's ball rolled off the green into a water hazard.

Mark removed his shoes and socks, rolled up his trousers, and waded into the water to look for his ball.

He found nine golf balls, but not a one of them was his.

Mark's ball was not lost, because he had it marked on the green. On the other hand, Mark's ball couldn't be played, because it was somewhere under the water.

The official called a two-stroke penalty on Mark, citing the rule that a player must finish the hole with the same ball he started with, unless his ball gets lost, of course—which is a penalty of one stroke and distance.

It was one of those times when common sense tells you one thing, but the law tells you something else.

At a National PGA Championship in Denver, a lady was sitting on a shooting stick behind a green, and an approach shot landed in her lap.

She looked shocked for a moment. Then she jumped up, and the ball rolled about ten yards closer to the hole. It was up to me to make the ruling. The pro who hit the shot was in contention.

The question was: Did the ball hit her, or did it come to rest in her lap? If it hit her and bounced off, the pro could play from near the hole.

My sympathy was with him. But I ruled the ball came to rest in her lap. He had to drop his ball where she had been sitting and was left with a tough downhill chip to face.

On the ninth hole of the same tournament, Arnold Palmer's approach shot rolled across the green and well into the fringe. Some spectators who were drinking and betting caught Arnold's ball and tossed it back onto the green.

The question was: Where should Arnold take his drop?

Joe Dey and I discussed it. Joe said since we hadn't seen the ball stop, we should let Arnold drop where Arnold thought it should be. I couldn't see any other way to rule, either.

At another hole, a pro was way out in the deep rough with a bunker 50 yards in front of him. The grass was knee high.

The rule is, you can part the grass with your hands or club while you are looking for your ball, but once the ball is found you cannot part the grass again.

The pro found his ball and was getting ready to hit. But at address he couldn't see the ball anymore, it was so far down in the grass.

I saw him bend over and sort of stir the grass with his fingers, hoping for a glimpse of his ball.

This is a two-stroke penalty. I looked at the poor pro standing in the deep grass with an impossible shot and bills to pay, and I kept my mouth shut.

Lo and behold, the pro dug that ball out of that deep grass with a mighty blow and it sailed over the bunker and carried onto the green. He had such a joyful look. I just smiled and walked away.

Wilmer's Woes

WILMER ALLISON, great tennis player and coach, was devoted to the game of golf.

Late one afternoon, we were playing and we came to a par five. Wilmer hit a good drive down the middle. He hit a nice second shot right up in front of the green, just a short pitch away.

Wilmer shanked the pitch shot.

He walked around behind the bunker to play his next

shot, and he shanked it again. Now he was almost in back of the green as he set up for another pitch shot.

Again he shanked it.

This put Wilmer to the left of the green. He took a couple of practice swings, set up for his pitch—and shanked it again.

Four shanks in a row took Wilmer on a complete circle of the green and placed him back in the middle of the fairway.

We were all laughing—all except Wilmer, I mean—as he pulled out his putter and banged the ball onto the putting surface.

"Well, after all, Wilmer, it is the shank of the evening," someone said when we reached the next tee.

You can imagine where Wilmer's drive went.

The Power of Negative Thinking

DESPITE THAT LITTLE ADVENTURE, Wilmer Allison almost never lost a golf game, because he nearly always had it won by the time he left the first tee.

If you could beat Wilmer, he wouldn't play you. He would take you as his partner.

And all the way around, Wilmer would harp about his

terrible luck. To hear him tell it, he had the worst luck of anyone who ever played the game. Wilmer never got a good bounce or a prime lie. Every break went against him.

This was Wilmer's way of luring his opponents into a false sense of security, which often led them into a streak of bad breaks and misjudgments.

The truth was that underneath his complaining, Wilmer knew he was going to win. His negative thinking was just a trick.

I always told my players just to worry about their own games. If you listen to what your opponents say, you'll head down a lot of wrong roads.

The Champion

NOT ONLY DOES Mickey Wright have one of the best— many would argue that it is the *very* best—golf swings in history, she is one of the classiest people it has ever been my privilege to know as a friend and pupil.

When she was asked at age fifty-eight why she had chosen to live a quiet life rather than cashing in on her many titles and her Hall-of-Fame status, Mickey said:

"I have no interest in translating my name into a million dollars, or any amount. To me golf means one thing and always has: the pure pleasure I get from swinging a golf club."

Practice It First

WHEN DARRELL ROYAL was coaching our football team at the University of Texas, he wouldn't have called upon his boys to run a play that they had never practiced in a game.

I believe the golfer should never try to play a shot he hasn't practiced a good deal.

On a windy day, most average golfers will go out and try to hit a low ball into the wind, or a high ball with the wind, when in the course of regular events they never practice either of those shots.

The only time most average golfers try to hit a soft, high wedge over a bunker is when they are faced with this predicament during a round of golf. You don't see many average golfers out there practicing with their wedges.

Much better for you to learn different shots on the practice range rather than banging away at the same one hour after hour.

I do advise, however, that average golfers select one club, perhaps a 7-iron, and learn to love it like a sweetheart. Learn how far it goes. Learn to hit it high or low, to hook it or slice it.

An average golfer can build a decent game around one club.

Wrongheaded Husbands

ONE OF THE BIGGEST PROBLEMS with women golfers is their husbands.

A husband nearly always tells his wife she "raised up."

This unfortunate woman will try her best to "stay down." But she can't hit the ball from there. She will hit the ground in back of it, or her left arm will bend at impact.

The most common reason for raising up is consciously trying to stay down. You can't raise up unless you are down to begin with.

The woman should be thinking, "chin up, stand tall"— not "stay down."

It pains me to hear the terrible advice husbands constantly give their wives regarding golf.

For years, her husband loudly admonished Joan Whitworth, one of my favorite women pupils, to "keep your head still." He got her so locked up that I could hardly persuade her to make a free swing. Joan is a fine athlete, too. What a pity her husband, Harry, didn't keep his golfing wisdom to himself.

Children

I DON'T TRY to teach golf to children. What they need is someone who will guide their learning. Let them play, then help them when they want you to, or when you see something that demands a teacher's attention.

Crosshanders

THE FIRST TIME they pick up a golf club and swing it, most children do it crosshanded. A right-handed child will put the left hand below the right hand on the grip.

I believe the reason is that instinctively a child knows that to hit a ball with a golf club, the left arm must be straight at impact. Pick up a club and try a slow crosshanded swing and you will see what I mean.

For a righthander, there is no way the left arm can keep from being straight at impact in a crosshanded swing. The left arm will bend in the backswing, but it will straighten as it comes down.

In the orthodox golf swing, with the left hand above the right on the grip, the left arm can all too easily break down through impact. This is a common mistake of poor players.

Most children will begin to copy adults and give up the crosshanded swing early. But some just keep on swinging crosshanded.

For a couple of summers I escaped the Texas heat and enjoyed myself as guest instructor at Cherry Hills in Denver. My son, Tinsley, was an assistant at the Pinehurst club across town. It was a very pleasant time for me.

At Cherry Hills I received a stipend for teaching that allowed me the freedom to spend as much time, or as little, as I thought each pupil needed. If I thought I had done all I could do for a pupil in ten minutes, I just moved on. On the other hand, I could spend all day with a pupil if I wished. This is my favorite way to teach.

I met a fine young assistant pro named Buddy Phillips at Cherry Hills. Buddy loved to teach, and he loved to practice. He would practice like a machine, scraping over one ball after another and hitting them down the range.

I used to take the club out of Buddy's hands every so often just to make him stop.

"Athletes in other sports take a time-out," I would tell him. "Go sit on your bag for a while."

Buddy's son, Tracy, was a three-year-old golf prodigy as a crosshanded swinger. Tracy hit the ball blindfolded, it didn't matter. He couldn't miss.

Once the great trick shot artist Paul Hahn said to Tracy, "Now, watch the ball."

Tracy hit the ball while looking down the fairway. He

thought Paul Hahn meant to watch the ball while it was in flight.

Buddy bent down and whispered, "Mr. Hahn means watch the ball on the tee."

We must be very careful what we say to children in a learning situation.

Buddy asked me what he should do about Tracy's crosshanded swing. I advised him to let Tracy keep swinging the way that felt right to him. When Tracy grew older and realized he needed more distance to play with his peers, he would change on his own.

At the age of six, Tracy got a disease that causes a softening of the right hipbone. For the next two and a half years, Tracy played golf standing on his left leg with his right leg in a sling.

He would go around the putting green chipping and putting and hopping on one leg hour after hour.

At age nine, with his hip disease abated, Tracy finally asked his dad if he should continue playing cross-handed.

Buddy picked up a sleeve of new Titleists and a sleeve of new Maxflis and walked out to the tee with his son.

Buddy said, "Hit three crosshanded and three ortho-dox, and we'll see which go the farthest."

The balls were longer with an orthodox swing, so Tracy changed over.

Except for chipping and putting. He continued to chip and putt crosshanded—which I would suggest any-one should try. The left wrist stays firm with a cross-handed chip or putt.

Another thing Tracy did as a youngster that I would

recommend is that he chipped and putted while looking at the hole, not at the ball.

This is a wonderful way to develop touch. You don't look at the basketball when you shoot a free throw, you look at the rim.

I mean, you should try looking at the hole in practice. But Tracy did it while playing, too.

At age fifteen, Tracy came to me for lessons. He was already a wonderful player and had one of the best short games I ever saw.

Tracy won the National Junior and the World Cup Junior and about eighty more junior tournaments.

Now Tracy is a teaching pro in Dallas—and a very good one, I would bet—and his dad, Buddy, is head pro at Cedar Ridge, a big, prosperous club in Tulsa.

The lesson for us all is, if you see children swinging golf clubs crosshanded, let them be. They're just doing what comes naturally.

The Left Arm

KEEPING THE LEFT arm straight at the top is not a requirement for a good swing.

But the left arm absolutely must be straight at impact.

The Secret of the
Golf Swing

WHEN AUSTIN COUNTRY CLUB was located on Riverside Drive, I was walking from the parking lot toward the shop when I heard my name being screamed from the direction of the practice area.

"Harvey! Harvey! I've got it! Eureka! I've found the secret!"

It was a member I had been teaching off and on for years with only fair success.

"I've found the secret of the golf swing, Harvey! I can't believe it's so simple!"

I said, "Please let me in on it. What is the secret of the golf swing?"

The member grew very solemn and owl-eyed with excitement.

"The secret is that the golf swing is just like hitting a ball with a stick!"

"Really?" I said, trying not to smile. I remembered the famous teacher, Percy Boomer, who was told by a pupil, "Percy, you teach it backwards. You say I should drive like I putt. The truth is, I must putt like I drive."

My pupil said, "It's as clear as can be. Like the sun

96

coming up to light the darkness. I can forget technical stuff and just swing the club as if I were hitting a ball with a stick. That's all there is to it. I don't know why you pros should make such a mystery of it."

I said, "Well, now that you have learned the secret, I guess you have no more need for a teacher."

My pupil said, "Thanks, Harvey. That's big of you."

This pupil moved to a different city a few months later and never contacted me again. Once the secret was learned, I suppose it stuck.

Hit It Hard

VERY EARLY in our time together I try to get my pupils to hit the ball hard, even with the short irons.

I believe if you start off in the game hitting the ball easy, you generally will keep it up. Your muscles learn the slow pace. You will always lack distance.

Sometimes it takes longer to unlearn than it does to learn.

Brand-Name Aiming

GOLFERS ON ALL LEVELS have been taught the trick of lining up their putts and then placing their golf balls down with the brand name aligned in the direction the putt should go.

It seems to me this is vaguely illegal. You can't lay a club on the green to use as an alignment guide. You can't aim a putt at your caddie's foot if it indicates the line.

But I don't know how a rule against this practice would ever be enforced. And I think the brand-name alignment does little, if any, good. In fact, it might be more of a distraction than an aid.

I believe your mind should be on the cup and on your touch rather than on the brand name of your golf ball.

The brand-name alignment is supposed to relieve your mind so you can concentrate on distance, but I think it often works in reverse.

Also, a common thing for the average player is to kneel down and line up the brand name, then stand up and look down and get the visual illusion that the brand name is lined up wrong. This really confuses matters.

Most players on every level do pretty well at aiming their putts. It is the touch for distance that separates the good putter from the not so hot.

Slices and Hooks

WHEN I MEET a new pupil who hits a hook, I know I am in for an easy time of it. I may not need to spend more than ten minutes with this pupil.

But when my pupil is a slicer, we are facing problems that may seem insurmountable. If you are hitting a slice, you are not going to get any better as a player. The more you swing, the bigger your slice becomes.

I don't see how a habitual slicer could really have a true sensation of how the game is played.

The first thing I set out to teach a new pupil who slices is how to hit a hook.

This may take a while.

But once the slicer has learned to hook, I can cure the hook quickly.

A pupil recently wrote me, "I know this is an unanswerable question, but I'll ask it anyway: What can I do about my slice? What's the first thing to try to fix? What's the most likely cause? Is there any salvation for a poor soul like me?"

Sure there is. Another teacher sent me a slicer with a note that said, "Harvey, if you can cure this person's slice, you can raise the dead."

This is what we did:

First, we used a 7-iron and made sure the pupil had as

99

strong a grip as looked reasonable. We made the pupil's V's point pretty much toward the right shoulder. I say I like to see a three-knuckle grip. But I don't like to see a pupil always looking down and trying to count knuckles. Just aim the V's generally toward the right shoulder, which will give you a three-knuckle grip.

Second, we squared the pupil's feet, hips, and shoulders to the line of flight. We made certain the pupil was not subconsciously allowing for a slice. Allow for a slice, and you will hit one.

Third, we played baseball.

I mean, we stood at home plate and aligned the pupil squarely with the pitcher's mound and second base.

Then we hit the ball over the shortstop.

We rolled the left forearm, not the wrist, to hit the ball.

The reason we hit the ball over the shortstop is so the pupil would not try to hit from the inside out. We want the ball hit from inside to square to inside.

But don't think about why. Just square up to the pitcher's mound and second base, then hit the ball over the shortstop with a 7-iron.

The pupil who came to me with the note about raising the dead now has a big hook, but is happy with being in the left rough at last. For a lifelong slicer, the left rough seems like a wonderful place to be—for a while.

Pretty soon, we'll have to cure that hook.

Pressure

DURING MY THIRTY-THREE YEARS as golf coach at the University of Texas, not only did I rarely travel to an out-of-town match with my teams, I didn't walk the course with them when they were playing matches here in Austin.

Usually I would watch them tee off on the first hole and then I would see them pass through at the ninth, tenth, and eighteenth.

I remember one match when I hid in the locker room and peeped out the curtain to see if my captain sank a vital three-foot putt on the final hole. He made it, and when I went outside to congratulate him, he said, "I knew you were in there."

Traveling with the teams was out of the question, because I had my hands full as head pro at Austin Country Club. But why didn't I walk along and observe their home matches?

My thinking was that my presence would only increase the pressure that my players already felt.

We had a quarterback at Texas named Bobby Layne who thrived on pressure. With the crowd screaming and everybody going crazy, Coach Blair Cherry could clap him on the shoulder and say, "Bobby, go in there and get us a score." Bobby would respond with a tremendous effort that often was successful.

But imagine me grabbing one of my golfers by the arm and saying, "We're depending on you, kid. Step up there and make that ten-foot putt!"

I always asked basketball coaches what they said to players who faced a crucial free throw that would win or lose the game. That's the closest comparison I can think of to a crucial golf shot.

In golf there is nobody to block for you or catch a pass. Like the free-throw shooter, you are alone with your mind, your heart, and your muscles.

Most basketball coaches said they told their players, "Just be yourself." Now and then a coach would say he told them, "The whole game is on your shoulders. You've got to come through!"

The best answer I got was from coaches who said, "You must know your players well enough to know how pressure affects each one of them."

When Betsy Rawls was a student at the University of Texas—the university did not have a women's golf team in her days there—I asked her if I would be a better coach if my players were afraid of me, as if I were a priest or a military officer. Betsy didn't have a team to play for, but she was entering tournaments and training for the Hall of Fame.

Betsy is a brilliant person, a Phi Beta Kappa in physics. If she hadn't become a golf champion, she could have been at the top of any field she chose.

She thought a long time and said, "No, not in your case. Your players know you get up early in the morning and go to bed late at night thinking about us. We know you're always available for instruction. That's all we need."

Dave Williams was a very successful golf coach at the University of Houston. Dave didn't play golf or teach it, but he knew how to recruit good players and keep them on a fine competitive edge, even if turning up the pressure was his answer.

Some golfers play just as well or even better than normal when the pressure is hot, and some fall apart.

The reason I want children to hole out every putt—no gimmes—and have something at stake on every hole, even if it is something imaginary, is so they will grow up accustomed to making shots under pressure.

I have seen players who can be thrown off their games by the slightest thing. Even the greatest can get their nerves tuned so tightly that a simple matter upsets them. I remember a tournament where a spectator's shadow fell across the line of Tommy Bolt's putt. Tommy looked at the sky and cried, "Lord, how can a man be expected to make a putt in the dark?"

I'm not sure which P. G. Wodehouse story it was, but I always laugh when I think of one of the characters who was too distracted to hit his shot because butterflies in the adjoining meadow were creating such a hullabaloo.

The Erratics

MANY GOOD PLAYERS continue to fire and fall back from success on the professional tour because they seem incapable of putting good rounds back to back.

Champions must string four good rounds together, or at least three. But the players I call the Erratics are not champions, and their names soon disappear from the sports pages.

Each Erratic is an individual, to be sure, and there is no one explanation why they continue to follow a 68 with a 77.

I believe, however, if I were trying to make a living playing golf I would keep a diary.

In my diary I would note such things as, Did I go out to dinner? What did I eat? Who was I with? What did we talk about? Did I drink spirits? How much did I sleep, and how well?

How did I feel physically? Was I tired? Did I have a head cold? How did I feel emotionally? Was I upset about something? Was I being cranky about small things? Or was my mind clear and my heart serene? Was my energy high? Was it low?

I would note what score I shot that day, the number of putts, and general comments on the all-around condition of my game.

Probably I would fill out my diary the last thing before bed. One thing for certain, I would never skip a night of writing in my diary.

What good would a diary do me as a professional golfer?

I feel that by periodically studying my diary, I would see patterns emerge.

My diary might show, for example, that I played better on days after I had eaten spaghetti for dinner with a couple of amusing pals and then watched a funny movie on television before lights out.

It could show, as well, whether spaghetti, companionship, and comedy were a prelude to disaster for me on the golf course.

There is no predicting what the diary might show, which is why keeping the diary is important.

The diary is the only suggestion I could give to an Erratic.

You don't lose your swing between the ninth green and the tenth tee, and you don't lose your swing from one day to the next. If you think you do, something is going on that you don't understand.

A diary might explain it to you.

How to Stop
the Bleeding

ALL GOOD PLAYERS reach patches in the midst of rounds when their games go awry.

I'm not talking about the habitual Erratics. I mean consistent, good players who for no apparent reason start making a string of bogeys, maybe a double bogey or two. They call it "bleeding." They ask me, "How can I stop the bleeding?"

As I always say of good players, you don't lose your swing between the green and the next tee, or between the tee and the approach shot.

The bleeding may be caused by bad breaks, which you simply must cope with. You should make birdies with your good breaks, but your bad breaks must not be allowed to mess up your thinking and poison your attitude.

Leaving breaks out of it, what causes the bleeding is what is going on in your mind during that five or ten minutes between shots.

While walking from your drive to your approach, is your mind caught up in considering results? Are you thinking ahead to future holes? For example, perhaps you are thinking, "I'll knock this wedge stiff for a birdie, then par that long, hard hole, reach the 17th in two for a cinch birdie—and par on the final hole will pay me a great, big fat check!"

Not only are you living too far in the future to be playing a sharp game of golf, you have let the thought of gold enter your mind. There may be gold and riches awaiting you, but not if you have started dreaming about them. You reach your reward stroke by stroke. You must be mindful of each stroke as it is played. Golf is played in the present.

If you can wash your mind clean each time while walking to your next shot, you have the makings of a champion.

That's what I mean by taking dead aim. I mean clearing the mind of all thoughts except the thought of the target, so that the muscles are free to do the job.

A good player's muscles do what they are told to do if they are free to do it.

Now let's suppose you are struggling with getting your mind on the job at hand, but nothing helps. You just can't do it. You can't stop the bleeding. What do you do?

You take it to the Lord in prayer—that is my best answer.

The Dashing Demaret

AT OUR ORIGINAL Austin Country Club—the first of our three locations—the dashing young Jimmy Demaret walked into the shop one day and asked me to play a round with him.

"I'm working on something in my swing. Let's go see how I'm doing with it," he said.

In later years, as he went on to win three Masters championships, Jimmy became a little plump and was famous for his colorful style of dressing, which attracted many fans to the game.

But on the day I am speaking of, Jimmy was thin and wiry, with big, strong forearms and powerful hands. I had powerful hands myself, from years of grinding and buffing clubs, but I wasn't as strong as Jimmy by any means.

Jimmy also was one of the most handsome fellows ever born and had a quick wit that stood him well in the company of such wits as Bob Hope and Bing Crosby.

Even as a young man, my face had already begun to wrinkle from sun and wind and, I suppose, something in my genes. Jimmy used to say, "Harvey, I could pour a bucket of water on your head, and not a drop of it would reach the ground."

Anyhow, Jimmy and I set out for a round of golf on the original Austin Country Club course.

"What is it you are trying to do with your swing?" I asked him on the tee.

He said, "I am trying to keep my elbows out in front of me on my follow-through."

I watched his swing intently that day, but I didn't get to see it very often.

Jimmy shot 30-29—59.

Ever since, keeping the elbows out in front on the follow-through has been one of the things I emphasize in teaching.

Luck

WHEN TOMMY KITE chipped into the hole at the seventh for a birdie two on the last round of the U.S. Open at Pebble Beach, was it luck—or was it the perfectly struck shot?

Or was it so nearly the perfectly struck shot that it gave luck a chance to happen?

When I give encouragement to someone, I say, "Play well" instead of "Good luck."

Sweet but Incomplete

ONE OF THE BEST SWINGERS we ever had on our golf team at the University of Texas was a boy named Ray Leggett. He hit the ball like a pro.

But there was a quirk in Ray's makeup that kept him from having a career in golf.

He hardly ever finished a round. Ray would tee off with three other boys, but somewhere along the way Ray would hit a shot he considered less than his best—and he would quit and walk back to the clubhouse, leaving his mates as a threesome.

Ray loved to practice. He could lay a towel on the ground down the range and stand there and hit 4-irons that landed on the towel all afternoon.

But he demanded too much of himself on the golf course. At the first sign of what he considered a poor shot, Ray was finished playing for the day.

Ray was a sweet boy. He didn't want to make a mistake. He lived on the practice tee.

Nothing I could say to him would change his mind.

Davis Love, Jr., was one of our players at that time. Davis wanted to be a teacher, not a touring pro. He loved to watch me giving lessons to a sweet swinger like Leggett.

During a session I noticed Ray had started regripping

the club at the top of his backswing. This is a bad habit that is easy to fall into, but difficult for a teacher to point out.

So as Ray reached the top of a swing, I grabbed the shaft of his club and stopped him. I did this in order to show Ray what he was doing. Davis observed closely.

That night in the dorm, the boys were talking golf and swinging clubs. Davis noticed that his roommate, Ed Turley, had begun regripping his club at the top.

Davis told Ed to make another swing.

As Ed's club started down, Davis grabbed it—a split second too late.

The sudden stop broke a bone in Turley's left wrist and put him out of golf for the season.

Even with a broken wrist, Ed played about as many rounds as Ray did.

Paula Granoff's Story

I HAD BEEN PLAYING golf for more than thirty years, but I wasn't enjoying the game anymore.

It was becoming a chore, really, just a whole bunch of work.

I had been to see nearly every famous golf teacher in the world except Harvey Penick. I certainly knew who

Harvey was, but I felt I would never be fortunate enough to take lessons from him. I thought he had retired and stopped teaching many years ago.

My husband, Lenny, and I are year-round golfers. We spend the winter at our home in Palm Beach, Florida, and the summer at our home in Providence, Rhode Island. I play almost every day, rain or shine. Lenny is not quite the golf nut I am. He won't play if the rain is really pouring hard.

Late in the spring of 1992, Lenny and I were driving from Palm Beach to Rhode Island. My back was hurting. I had been working in Florida with two famous teachers. One told me my swing was too flat, and we worked on it. The other told me my posture was all wrong, and we worked on it. He wanted me to stay bent over through the entire swing and keep my left arm straight. After two months with that guy, I thought I had broken my back.

Cruising along the highway, I was sort of listening to the radio, thinking about one thing and another—and I heard a voice saying Harvey Penick had written a book that had just been published.

I told Lenny, "Phone our book store and tell them I must have that book. We're going to stop at the book store before we even go to our house."

That night I sat down and read Harvey's book from cover to cover.

First thing the next morning, I went out to the barn and found a weed cutter, just as Harvey had said to do.

I started swinging the weed cutter as if it were a golf club.

Right away I knew something different and wonderful was happening.

I picked up my 6-iron and swung it like the weed cutter.

Voilà! This was it! For the first time in my life, I understood how a golf swing was supposed to feel.

It was like I had discovered electricity.

Well, I spent the next four or five days swinging that weed cutter and then swinging my 6-iron and then swinging the weed cutter again—and then I entered the Rhode Island State Seniors.

I had been a decent player—not much distance, good short game—but I had never won anything to speak of. I was medalist at a tournament once. I reached the semi-finals of another tournament.

So with two thoughts in my mind—swing the weed cutter and clip off the tee—I went on to win the Rhode Island State Seniors championship.

Not only did I win it, I won it handily.

One of my competitors told me during the tournament that she had read Harvey's book, and she thought it was a bunch of bull. I just nodded and smiled and silently hoped she kept on thinking that until I had beaten her.

I don't need to tell you how thrilled I was.

I thought, well, if I can improve so much with just this simple act of swinging the weed cutter and clipping the tee, I had best try to go see Harvey in person. I wanted to meet him. I wanted him to look at my grip and stance, and I wanted to hear him speak.

I phoned and talked to Helen, a wonderful person

who has become a warm friend to me, and it was arranged that Lenny and I would come to Austin and Harvey would watch me hit some balls.

That first morning at Austin Country Club, I met Helen and Harvey's son, Tinsley, the head pro. Tinsley warned me his dad might not be feeling well, and he might not spend much time with me. But I thought, well, at least I'll get to meet the man, and I can tell my friends about it.

Tinsley took me to the practice tee to wait for his dad. I noticed a kid on the range, a little boy with big eyeglasses and a gorgeous swing.

"That boy has talent," I said.

"Yes, that's Paul Kite, Tom's son," Tinsley said.

I guess it's in the genes.

Harvey arrived at the practice tee in a golf cart driven by his attractive young nurse. Golf carts are not allowed on the practice tee except in Harvey's case. A special entrance has been cleared for Harvey's cart. A sign declares that this entrance is for Harvey Penick only.

Harvey looked very dapper that morning in his Scottish-style golf cap, a light sweater, sharply creased trousers and polished alligator shoes. His body is frail and he is in constant pain from arthritis, though he never shows it in public. His face is wrinkled from age and from decades in the sun, but a kind of glow shines out of him. You feel at once that you are in the presence of someone rare.

We chatted for a few minutes.

He said, "I'm flattered that you would come all the way from Rhode Island to see me. I sure hope I don't disappoint you too much."

Then he said, "Take off your glove."

I didn't understand.

He repeated, "Please take off your golf glove. I want to see your grip."

I might say here that during the lesson Harvey forgot to tell me to put my glove back on. Later he said one of his most common errors is forgetting to tell his pupils to put their gloves back on. I think he might do it on purpose. At any rate, I have never worn a golf glove again.

Anyway, I removed my glove that first morning and Harvey looked at my grip.

He turned my hands a little to the right, making my grip stronger.

I said, "Harvey, before we start I want to tell you that my swing is too flat."

He said, "Let's try squaring up your left foot a little."

I said, "And I don't get enough distance."

He said, "It's all fixed now."

"What do you mean?" I said. "How could it be fixed?"

He said, "Changing your grip got rid of the flat. Moving your foot got rid of the short. Now make me a swing and clip off that tee."

I hit a beautiful ball with good distance that fell to the earth with a slight draw.

"I hope you enjoyed that as much as I did," Harvey said.

I was astonished that it was so easy. I hit one beautiful shot after another. But I started thinking, well, gosh, he hasn't really told me anything.

I asked him where my club should be at the nine o'clock position.

Harvey said, "Forget about it. The toe of your club is

pointing straight up at waist level, so you are doing fine. I just want you to place your hands on the club as I have showed you, square up your left foot, and clip off the tee."

I realized I needed to discard all my old thoughts about mechanical positions. Instead I needed to think like an athlete. It was like I was throwing a ball.

After a while, Harvey said, "That's enough."

But I was hitting the ball so well that I wanted to hit a few more.

Harvey said, "Let's leave well enough alone."

As I came to know him I learned that when he says, "Leave well enough alone," he means it. To him you are finished with whatever it is you are doing.

About that time I was startled to see a woman come through the hedges and stroll onto the tee, carrying a big silver trophy in her arms.

She walked over to Harvey, and I heard her say, "Tom says this belongs to you," or something of that nature.

And it struck me: My gosh, this is the U.S. Open Trophy that Tom Kite had won two days ago at Pebble Beach!

This was Tom Kite's wife, Christy, giving the U.S. Open Trophy to Harvey!

What a moving thing it was to see.

After the celebration, Harvey and I went to the practice green.

I put down three balls. I made the first putt. I made the second putt.

Harvey said, "That's enough."

I said, "I'll just stroke this third putt."

Harvey said, "No need for that. You have a good touch. I'm not going to mess with your putting."

I thought, well, all these years I have been going to teachers who behave like brain surgeons, and now I have put myself in the hands of a medicine man.

That seemed to be the end of the lesson for the day, but actually it wasn't.

In the afternoon Lenny and I went to visit Helen at the Penick home near the country club. Harvey was sitting in his favorite chair. I mentioned to him that Lenny and I both had trouble in sand traps beside the green.

Harvey gave us a lesson right there on the rug.

He said to stand facing the hole with the blade of the sand wedge open so that it aimed to the right. Then he said to move our left feet to the left so that the wedge aimed at the hole. He said to let our shoulders and hips follow the lead of our left feet.

"Now just make a normal swing and cut the sand out from under the ball and knock it into the cup," he said.

Of course, we couldn't swing our wedges on Helen's rug. So Lenny and I rushed back over to the country club and went to the practice bunker—and once again it worked! I have never feared a bunker since.

Now I phone Helen two or three times a week. Sometimes I ask Harvey for a tip, but he won't give me one unless I promise I have had trouble three rounds in a row. Lenny and I stop off in Austin to see the Penicks as we are going and coming between Palm Beach and Providence. Tinsley and his wife, Betty Ann, have visited in our home in Rhode Island. We've all become friends.

My four-year-old grandson is learning golf. I cut

down a club for him. He makes the same motion as swinging a weed cutter. I make him clip the tee five times before I will put a ball on it.

I know that this way of teaching works. There's no use in my grandson treading water for thirty years like I did.

Indoor Teaching

MY OLD FRIEND Bob McDonald leased a building on State Street in Chicago, hired five teaching pros, and started an indoor golf school.

The school attracted a large number of pupils who were eager to hit golf balls and work on their swings in the bitter Chicago winter.

Bob told me he had one pupil who arrived several times a week and spent hours hitting balls into the net. Bob watched the fellow closely. Near as Bob could tell under the circumstances, this pupil was making good progress.

But when spring came, the pupil returned to his golf club only to discover that over the winter he had developed a terrible snap hook that barely got into the air.

The famous teacher Ernest Jones taught mostly indoors in New York City and apparently did quite well. And I do sympathize with the millions of golfers who live in areas where winter snows cover the ground. I know how powerful the urge to hit golf balls is—even if you have to hit them into a net indoors.

Many pupils send me photographs, films, and videotapes of their swings and ask me to help them by looking at pictures.

This is even more difficult than it would be to help by watching them hit balls into a net.

If I am teaching you, I must see whether I am going to apply myself to your swing or to the angle of your clubface. You could have the best-looking swing in the country, but the angle of your clubface could be off by three degrees, and I couldn't tell unless I could see the flight of the ball for a distance.

In order to help I must watch your ball flight and I must see your divot. I can do neither of those if you hit the ball off a mat into a net.

For golfers in colder climates, I suggest you get a heavy practice club and swing it daily to keep your golfing muscles in shape through the winter (I suggest swinging a heavy club for all golfers in any sort of climate, in fact). Swing a heavy club in the winter, and you will hit the ball farther in the spring.

But I am not telling you to stay away from indoor driving ranges. Even in the best of weather, golfers in big cities often don't have time to go to a golf course, or even have a golf course to which they can go.

If the urge to hit golf balls becomes overwhelming, as it frequently does, then by all means head for the indoor range. But look upon it as recreation and as satisfying a golf addiction.

Beware of grooving bad habits with an indoor swing.

Masters Manners

AT THE MASTERS, spectators are provided with a course map that includes pairings, starting times, and a note from Bobby Jones which says:

> In golf, customs of etiquette and decorum are just as important as rules governing play. It is appropriate for spectators to applaud successful strokes in proportion to difficulty, but excessive demonstrations by a player or his partisans are not proper because of the possible effect on other competitors.
>
> Most distressing to those who love the game of golf is the applauding or cheering of misplays or misfortunes of a player. Such occurrences have been rare at the Masters, but we must eliminate them entirely if our patrons are to continue to merit their reputation as the most knowledgeable and considerate in the world.
>
> No matter how well you may know a player, do not accost him on the golf course. Give him a chance to concentrate on his game. Walk—never run. Be silent and motionless when a contestant prepares to execute a stroke. Be considerate of other spectators.

A Golfer's Poem

I DON'T KNOW if Robert Service was a golfer, but he wrote a poem that competitive players should memorize.

The poem is named "The Quitter":

It's easy to cry when you're beaten
  and die
It's easy to crawfish and crawl.

But to fight and to fight when hope's out of sight
  Ah, that's the best game of all.

And when you come out of each grueling bout
  all beaten and battered and scarred

Have one more try. It's dead easy to die.
  It's the keepin' on livin' that's hard.

Wasting Your Time

UNLESS YOU HAVE a reasonably good grip and stance, anything you read about the golf swing is useless.

Mr. Connerly

ONE OF OUR MEMBERS, Bob Connerly, was Texas State champion four times and played golf at our club with President Taft in Austin just a little before my day.

Later I played golf with Mr. Connerly quite often. He told me President Taft was not an efficient golfer, but he did love the game. A bodyguard on horseback with a 30-30 rifle in a saddle holster followed them around the course.

Mr. Connerly was a remarkable fellow. His bag had five clubs in it—driver, a midiron, a niblick, a lofter, and a putter.

In modern terms this would be like carrying a driver, 2-iron, 5-iron, 9-iron, and putter.

Furthermore, Mr. Connerly played crosshanded.

Mr. Connerly called his putting stroke "the pendulum." He used his shoulders like a rocking chair.

Recently Sandra Palmer came to me for a putting lesson. I persuaded her to try the Connerly-crosshanded grip. I like it because it prevents the left wrist from breaking down.

Breaking the left wrist forward so that the blade passes in front of the hands is a deadly sin in putting.

Mr. Connerly was a wizard of a putter. His crosshanded swing cost him distance, but his shots went where he aimed them.

He used a large-size golf ball called the Black Domino.

Mr. Connerly was also the state skeet champion. He would have me hit shots with his Black Domino balls, and he would blast them out of the sky with his shotgun.

When I was a young pro, Mr. Connerly ordered me to round off the toe of his driver. I thought, well, there goes a good club ruined. But Mr. Connerly was at least two years ahead of the club designers. With his altered driver he could smack that Black Domino off our hard summer lies with amazing accuracy.

I noticed early that great players like Mr. Connerly in golf and Wilmer Allison in tennis had something in their eyes that normal people don't have. They saw things the rest of us can't see.

Fate Takes a Hand

IT WAS A CRISP MORNING in May, and the Southwest Conference golf championship was on the line.

As the University of Texas coach, I sent my four best players—Morris Williams, Jr., Marion Pfluger, Wesley Ellis, and Billy Penn—to Fort Worth to play undefeated TCU at one of the finest golf courses in the world, Colonial Country Club.

From its inception Colonial has been rated the top course in Texas, or very close to it. But in the days of this match I am about to describe, Colonial was even tougher than it is today. Storms and floods have destroyed many of Colonial's giant oaks, and architectural decisions have pulled some of the teeth that the original designer, my friend John Bredemus, put into the layout.

I am not diminishing the Colonial of today. It is a great course. But forty years ago—when Colonial was known as Hogan's Alley—it was tighter and harder than it is now.

My number-one player, Morris Williams, Jr., had lost only one match in his life. That was when Harvie Ward, the best amateur in the world for ten years, beat Morris 1-up in the 36-hole NCAA final in 1949.

Morris had beaten Billy Maxwell, Don January, Earl Stewart, Don Cherry, Joe Conrad, Buster Reed, and the

Cupit brothers, among others, during his brief career that was to be ended soon in a plane crash.

We needed to win at Colonial to assure Texas another SWC title. So I matched Morris against the TCU captain, a tall, slender, cocky sophomore named Dan Jenkins.

This Jenkins boy was not only a full-time student at TCU, he was also a full-time sports writer for *The Fort Worth Press*.

From the tips Colonial played more than 7,000 yards and looked twice as long. As a concession to the members, who were generous to allow college teams to compete there, the TCU and Texas squads started on the back nine first.

Morris had never seen Colonial, but he later told me that Jenkins, with whom he had become friendly, was nice enough to point out every danger and pitfall that Morris might have overlooked.

On the tee Jenkins would say, "You want to stay left here . . . a creek comes in over there . . . this next green is slick as a glacier."

No doubt Jenkins was trying to mess up Morris's mind. But that sort of needling never worked with Morris. With his pants cuffs turned up a couple of times, and a repeating upright swing, Morris almost never missed a fairway or green. When Morris had a 9-iron or wedge in his hand, he expected to hit it stiff. Morris played with incredible confidence, the kind that comes from knowing you'll have to be under par to beat him. Morris was grinning and friendly, almost apologetic about how good he was.

After 15 holes Williams and Jenkins were even par and level in the match.

Ben Hogan and Marvin Leonard, the mercantile king whose imagination and money built Colonial, drove up in a golf cart to watch them.

Morris was greatly impressed. He asked Dan, "Does Hogan follow you guys much?"

"Oh, sure, all the time," Jenkins said.

At Colonial's seventh hole—the 16th of their match—Jenkins pushed a 1-iron off the tee into the right rough behind some trees. Morris hit a 3-wood down the middle.

Jenkins had a shot if he could hook a high 6-iron over the trees and hit it far enough to reach the green. With Hogan watching, Jenkins hit perhaps the best shot he would ever hit in his life. The ball came to rest six inches from the cup for a cinch birdie. This birdie would have put Jenkins 1-up on Morris with two holes to play.

From back down the fairway, Morris pulled out a 7-iron, settled into that square stance of his—and hit the ball into the cup for an eagle!

Deeply shaken, Jenkins 3-putted the next hole and lost the match, 2-and-1.

Texas had won another championship. Morris shot a 68, two under par, the one and only time he ever saw Colonial.

One year later in the Southwest Conference Tournament—a medal event that was played to establish the individual champion—this same Jenkins kid 3-putted sixteen times in 72 holes to finish third behind Buddy Weaver of Rice and Wesley Ellis of Texas.

Over the years, I have come to know Dan Jenkins as a friend as well as a famous sportswriter and novelist.

I like to tell him, "Well, Dan, think how lucky you are. If Morris hadn't holed out that 7-iron, and if you had 3-putted only twelve times at the tournament, you might today be an assistant pro at Goat Hills."

Unfair to Ben

IT ANNOYS ME TO HEAR the television commentators talking about Ben Crenshaw being a wild driver who is always in the rough and has to save himself with miraculous putting.

It's not just because I love Ben like my own son, either.

Ben is indeed one of the best putters who ever lived, right at the top beside Horton Smith.

And it is true that he can get down in two from the parking lot.

But it is not true that he is a wild driver compared to some of the outstanding players among his peers. This is just one of those things that some television announcers say and some sportswriters like to write because it would seem to be a colorful trait.

If you would pair Ben in a tournament with Davis Love III and Fred Couples, for example, I would bet my five dollars that Ben would be in the fairway as often as any of them.

Made in Heaven

AFTER HIS LATEST birthday, Charlie Crenshaw, Ben's father, remarked that he might be nearing the end of his golfing habit.

"When your forward press is longer than your backswing, you've got to think about giving up the game," Charlie said.

But I know Charlie too well to believe he will ever quit. He'll be asking St. Peter to make him a match.

Chipping

MANY PUPILS COME to me with the notion that their chipping stroke should be the same as their putting stroke.

They have been taught that from a few feet off the green, chipping with, say, a 7-iron, they should hit the ball just exactly as if it were a long putt. Some even use their putting grips.

But chipping is not like putting.

128

Think of a chip shot as a little drive, and of a drive as a big chip shot.

To take your putting grip, you weaken your left hand and strengthen your right. The object of this is to keep the putter blade square to your line.

For a chip shot, use your regular grip. But place your hands toward the bottom of the handle. Play the ball in the center of your stance. Lean slightly more weight on your left foot. Make a backswing and forward swing of the same length, as if you were tossing the ball under-handed. And, of course, keep your hands ahead of, or even with, the clubhead all the way through the shot, including the follow-through.

If your ball is a few feet off the green and you want to use your putter—what we call the Texas Wedge—then by all means use your putting stroke to go with it.

But unless you have a putter in your hands, you don't want to stroke the ball like a putt.

One good practice for chipping is to put your golf bag down about eight feet in front of you and then hit chip shots that bounce off the bag. At first you may find yourself hitting the ball over the bag, because you are trying to help the ball into the air. Keep at it until your shots bounce off the bag. It's the same idea as chipping beneath a bench.

From the edge of the practice green, don't stand and chip at the same hole over and over. Aim for holes of different distances. Touch is what you are trying to develop.

Probably the most common mistake among average players is trying to chip with too much loft. It requires the touch of an artist to hit a chip shot with a wedge. The average player should get his ball on the ground and rolling as soon as possible. Chip with the least lofted club that will do the job.

A strong chipper and putter has a good chance to beat anybody any time. As I used to tell my university players, "If your opponent keeps getting down in two from off the green and beats you, don't think it's luck."

What Do You Look At?

WHAT DO YOU look at when you look at the ball?

If I looked at the back of the ball, I would hook it.

If I looked at the top of the ball, a thin shot would be the result.

If I looked at the inside rear quarter of the ball, I would have too much to think about.

When I look at you, do I look at your eyes? Your nose? Your mouth? No, I am aware of these features, but what I see is the whole you.

And that's what I think you should see when you look at a golf ball. Be aware of the whole ball, but not intent on any one part of it.

Telephone Lesson

SANDRA PALMER PHONED our home and asked Helen to ask me to help her with her follow-through.

I could hardly see her follow-through over the long-distance line, and it was difficult for Sandra to try to describe it to Helen, who tried to describe it to me.

Finally I said, "The follow-through is a result of what has gone before it. Ask Sandra what her problem is with striking the ball."

Helen said, "She says she leaves too many shots out to the right."

I said, "Tell her to toe in her club a little before she places her hands on the grip."

This is the same thing as strengthening her grip, which I couldn't do unless I could see her hands on the club.

It's just an aspirin, not a cure. I felt like a doctor of a bygone era, when a person would call with an ailment and the doctor would say, "Take an aspirin and phone me tomorrow."

But I know that toeing-in the club would straighten her shot, and that would have to affect her follow-through.

Still the Most
Dreaded Shot

MY MAIL BRINGS many letters like this from a woman in Kansas City:

"Dear Harvey, I read your *Little Red Book* and gave special study to the chapter you call 'The Dreaded Four-Footer.'

"In my case, you could call it 'The Dreaded Three-Footer.' Or even 'The Dreaded Two-Footer.'

"The awful truth is that in our club wife-husband tournament last weekend, I had twenty-two 3-putts in 36 holes. I missed twelve putts of four feet or less.

"Harvey, I missed four putts of no more than one foot!

"And I was trying hard!

"I was doing exactly what you said to do on a short putt. I approached every putt from behind to see the line. I took one, two, or three practice strokes, concentrating on the line. Then I imitated my last practice stroke. I was careful not to look up and peek at the ball. I set my mind on stroking the putter on the sweet spot and on the line. I told myself, 'No negative thoughts.' I told myself, 'Forget the distance, just keep the putter blade square.'

"But they don't go in. I am putting worse than ever. My husband says I am crazy. What can I do?"

The woman's letter is a self-diagnosis.

She is thinking about the fundamentals while she is putting in a tournament.

The place to think about the fundamentals is on the practice green, over and over, hour after hour.

Your putting system must be automatic.

Many golfers become so involved in the process that they forget the goal—which is the bottom of the cup.

There are two good reasons why the three- or four-foot putt is the most dreaded shot in the game for so many average golfers once they get into some kind of tournament.

The most obvious reason is that average golfers never practice three- or four-foot putts. Oh, they will hit a couple before they tee off, but missing them may do more harm than good. I mean, how many average golfers do you see standing on the practice green for hours knocking in three-foot putts? The answer is: None. Only pros and top amateurs seriously practice three-footers.

The other reason, I think, is "gimmes." Many average players will practically get down on their knees and beg to be given a two-footer in a friendly game.

Much better to putt them all and not play under the illusion that two-footers are "good."

That's like thinking the banker will stamp your note "paid in full" if you are only a few dollars short.

Reassurance

MARK BEDELLION, a medical student who played golf for the University of Texas, used to be a puzzle to me. I would see him hitting balls at the club, and he looked good enough to be a winner on the pro tour. Then I would read in the newspaper that he had shot 80 in some amateur tournament.

Finally he came to me for a lesson.

"I'm glad you're here, Mark," I said. "I've been wondering what your problem could be."

"I can tell you the answer to that easily enough," he said. "My swing is too flat. I need to swing more upright. It's what everybody tells me."

I said, "Son, Ben Hogan had a flat swing. Nobody ever had a flatter swing than Lee Trevino. What I want you to do is forget what everybody tells you. Use the swing God has blessed you with, and go play golf. Right now."

Mark went to the back tees at our beautiful, but difficult, Pete Dye course—full of canyons and water hazards, pot bunkers and lovely vistas—and shot a 68.

In the early years of our new course we had only two members who could play that well—Tommy Kite and Ben Crenshaw.

Mark continued with his medical career, but he still plays a fine game of golf. Like so many golfers, his main problem was that he needed to have confidence in his swing.

A Future in Golf

ONE OF OUR MEMBERS, George McCall, mentioned to me that a former Texas player, Martin Alday, had won the championship at Midland Country Club. George told me Martin's caddie was a sharp kid who probably had a good future in golf. George asked if we could find a summer job at our club for the kid, and would I give him some lessons instead of paying him a wage?

That is how I met Terry Jastrow.

Terry was about sixteen, a blond, good-looking boy, full of enthusiasm. I don't know what he expected when he showed up for work, but the first thing he got was a lecture.

"A lot of you Midland boys have daddies in the oil business, and you think you can get things handed to you right away," I said. "But golf at your level has nothing to do with money. I am going to start with you at the beginning, with your grip and stance, and if you become a good player it will be step by step, and it might be very slow."

I put Terry to work as a bag boy, loading and unloading and cleaning clubs for the members.

In his off hours, I sent Terry to the opposite end of the practice range at our club on Riverside Drive. He thought he was a fair player already, but his grip was too strong to travel outside West Texas. I told Terry he could hit nothing but 9-irons. I told him to think of clipping the grass with a weed cutter.

Now and then I would go visit Terry at the far end of the range to see how he was doing. I would touch his hands and pick at the calluses. Terry had the habit of "motorcycling," twisting his hands onto the grip rather than placing them there. This is the main cause for calluses.

About the time Terry would think I had forgotten him, I would show up again and watch him for a while. Eventually he graduated from a 9-iron to a 7-iron. It was several weeks before I let him hit a wood, and even then I took the driver out of his bag.

At the end of that first summer, Terry qualified for the championship flight of the state junior tournament and made it all the way to the finals before losing.

The next summer, Terry reported for work at Austin Country Club again. I set him to digging irrigation ditches.

He still had to practice at the far end of the range, but I let him play the course if it wasn't too crowded. He usually played with Tommy Kite and Barbara Puett.

That second summer, Terry won the state junior, beating John Mahaffey in the finals. Terry was medalist in the national junior and went to the quarterfinals before Lanny Wadkins knocked him out.

I thought Terry might enroll at the University of Texas, where his brother Kenny was already a student. But Terry's mind was set on being a golf pro, and the University of Houston had the dominant program in college golf at the time. Terry became a Houston Cougar.

136

Next thing I knew I saw a photo in *Sports Illustrated* of Terry being given a golf lesson by Houston coach Dave Williams. Williams was running a very successful program, but he didn't play golf or teach it, that I had ever heard of.

Terry showed up at Austin Country Club for lessons.

"I can't do it, Terry," I said. "I see that you are studying with Coach Williams, and I wouldn't want to tell you anything that might violate his teachings. One teacher at a time is plenty."

In his sophomore year, Terry went to work doing odd jobs for ABC-TV.

He told me, "I can't believe I will find a true source of happiness in needing to make five-foot putts week after week."

It turned out that Terry did indeed have a bright future in golf, but it was as a television producer and director rather than as a player.

And who do you think was producing the telecast when Tommy Kite won the U.S. Open at Pebble Beach?

Terry said, "When Tommy finally holed out, I was so full of joy that I took off my headset and went into an office by myself and wept for half an hour."

It took me that long just to get my toes uncurled.

The Sweet Spot

PUPILS THINK I'M CRAZY when I say this, but the sweet spot on the new oversize drivers that are all the rage at the moment is smaller than the sweet spot on the regular-size drivers.

By sweet spot, I mean the no-roll spot—the place on the clubface where a squarely struck ball is launched with no immediate spin to the left or right.

Let me explain it this way: If you want to drive a small nail into a board, would you select a big hammer or a small hammer?

With a small hammer you can hit the nail with any part of the head and drive it home. With a big hammer you have a larger area with which to hit the nail, but at the same time you have a greater risk of hitting the nail off-center and bending it.

I asked Victor East, the genius behind Spalding golf clubs, if the sweet spot for Sam Snead was the same as the sweet spot for me.

He said yes, sure it is.

I noticed, however, that Snead wore out his driving club—usually a brassie—a little on the toe. A hook is hit toward the toe, and Sam hooked every shot. Hitting the ball toward the toe meant he de-lofted his 12-degree brassie into probably eight or nine degrees with his swing.

Slices are hit in the heel, which also adds loft to the club.

I have been asked at PGA schools why Snead gripped the club so lightly and Arnold Palmer gripped it so tightly.

Snead could grip lightly because he hit the ball in the same spot every time. Palmer's tighter grip is to prevent the club from twisting on his hits that are less precise than Snead's.

What they call "perimeter weighting" is supposed to make the whole face of an oversize metal wood into a so-called sweet spot. But what it really does is put more weight behind mis-hit shots. It makes your misses greater, it seems to me. I believe your misses are better with a smaller-headed club.

But the oversize heads do seem to give people confidence, and that is worth a lot.

And if you do happen to hit an oversize driver on the sweet spot, I think you gain a little distance. The problem is finding the sweet spot in that large hunk of metal.

Playing Hurt

ALTHOUGH IT LOOKS like such a peaceful game, golfers are beset with all sorts of injuries from muscle sprains to bad backs, from torn rotator cuffs to broken bones.

The one thing an injured golfer wants to know first is, "How can I keep playing?"

A friend sprained his left ankle on the second tee on the first day of a golfing trip to Scotland. He hobbled off the course in agony at the ninth and had a doctor tape the sprained ankle in a splint. He played for two weeks in Scotland on the sprained ankle, and by the time he came home, he had torn a ligament in his right knee because of it.

He told me he was playing at Royal Musselburgh, limping along as well as he could, when a woman appeared and called his caddie aside for a brief warning chat.

"What does she want?" my friend asked when the woman left.

The caddie said, "She wants you to get off the golf course."

"But why? There's no one pressing behind us."

The caddie said, "Aye, but she says sooner or later the gimp won't be able to keep up."

My friend told his caddie, "From now on, you find all

my drives about 275 yards down the middle of the fairway." And he kept going.

If you have sore knees, they will be less painful if you wear rubber-sole shoes rather than spikes. In Scotland and England, where players walk, and walk fast, rubber-sole shoes are very popular.

A sore shoulder in the rotator cuff area is a common problem. You should ice it after you play. Exercise your shoulder often, swinging your arms in slow circles to keep your muscles from tightening.

Above all, you Seasoned Citizens especially, set aside a full five minutes to stretch before a round. If you don't have time both to stretch and hit practice balls, I suggest that you choose to stretch. Loosen up the grease, as Darrell Royal says. This will put you in shape to play much better than will rushing through a small bucket of balls.

The small bones of the hands are very susceptible to injuries, especially by good players who swing that club at upwards of 115 miles an hour.

Lee Trevino recently had surgery on his thumb. Ben Crenshaw had a sore left thumb and asked if I had any suggestion what he should do about it. I said he could try taking his left thumb off the handle in his grip, the way the great Henry Picard did. That's why Picard started gripping the club in that fashion—because of a thumb injury.

Ben tried it for a few swings and was free of pain. But I am happy to say he promptly returned to his regular grip, which is a thing of beauty.

Many golfers get back injuries from bending over the

wrong way to take the ball out of the cup. An orthopedist told me there would be far fewer back injuries if golfers would learn to sit down and cross one leg over the other to tie their shoes, instead of standing up straight and reaching down for the laces.

As golfers grow older they are subject to aches and pains of arthritis, bursitis, and other symptoms of aging. I know many who gulp down a handful of pain pills before they tee off.

Jack Nicklaus, Arnold Palmer, Tom Kite—the list goes on and on—have hurt their backs, but continue playing at the price of doing hours of exercises and stretching every day.

If you have just a minor, nagging injury that doesn't threaten to become a major one, there is one danger I can see if you keep on playing: A small hurt can take your mind off what it should be on—which is, taking dead aim.

The Feeling of Far

MANY TIMES over the years I have heard Byron Nelson say, "Just let it happen. Don't try to hit the ball far. Instead develop a feeling that the ball is going to go a long way without your really trying. And sure enough, it will."

In the Eyes

YOU SHOULD HAVE your eyes examined periodically, not only for the good of your life, but for the sake of your golf.

As pilots will tell you, your vision can change a bit from day to day. This is natural and nothing to be concerned about. It is the vision change that lasts that you must get corrected.

As you get older, you may become farsighted or nearsighted, but this is not always a sign of age. One of the finest junior players I ever taught, Tina Trimble, needed to wear glasses, but worried about the effect they would have on her appearance.

I reminded her that "Pretty is as pretty does"—a wise old saying that counts in everything in life.

Tina went on to play for a good team at Furman, where she was a straight-A student.

Most great players have sharp vision, even though it may be the result of eyeglasses or contact lenses.

Few good players wear dark glasses during a round. The reason I never wore them is that I felt I couldn't see well enough through tinted glass.

The best player I can think of who wore dark glasses in competition was the Canadian sweet swinger, George Knudson.

In the Mind

MY OLD FRIEND Don Massengale arrived at the club looking dejected. He hadn't been playing well on the Senior Tour. I kidded around with him, saying I had to turn the sports page upside down to find his name, but he was not amused.

"Let me watch you hit a few," I said.

Don borrowed a 3-wood from a member on the range. Don was wearing slick-sole loafers and bifocals, and the place he chose to hit from gave him a downhill lie.

He stood there and banged 3-woods, one after the other, straight down the middle about 240 yards. He never came close to missing one, and I never offered a word of advice.

All I could say to him was, "Don, anybody who can hit the ball as I have just seen you hit it had better go back out there and keep playing. There's nothing in your swing that should cause you to be in a slump."

With good players like Don, problems are nearly always mental.

A simple thing to remember, but a hard thing to grasp and do, is this—if you want to change yourself, you must change how you think.

Old Familiar

NORRIS WILLIAMS—not Morris, but Norris, a woman who has traveled widely with my wife, Helen—entered the pro shop one afternoon with a look of desperation on her face.

She said, "Harvey, I want to buy a new putter. This old one is no good anymore."

I said, "You know, I was talking to Mickey Wright about putters the other day. Mickey has an old cash-in model with a touch of lead tape on the toe and another bit of lead on the heel so that it feels very much like a Ping putter. Mickey has won eighty-two professional tournaments with that putter, and she still uses it."

"What are you trying to say?" asked Norris.

"Norris, it's not the fiddle, it's the fiddler."

Norris whirled around and walked out with her old putter in her hand. She still uses that putter today, many years later.

Governor Hobby

MY BIG BROTHER, Tom, was the number-one caddie at our club, and he nearly always carried the bag for Governor Bill Hobby, who was an enthusiastic golfer.

When World War I came along, Tom joined the Marines and went overseas to fight.

Many months after the war ended, I was in the caddie yard and heard my name being called. It was Governor Hobby.

"Harvey, where on earth is Tom?" he said.

"Sir, Tom is still in France, guarding German prisoners. It looks like he's never going to come home," I said.

Governor Hobby said, "Harvey, you get me the information on Tom and be at my office tomorrow morning."

The next morning I put on my best hand-me-downs and went to the State Capitol Building. Several important-looking men were sitting in the lobby outside the Governor's office. I took a seat with them.

The office door opened. Governor Hobby came out. All the important-looking men and the skinny kid in hand-me-downs jumped to their feet.

"Harvey, come into my office," Governor Hobby said, putting an arm around my shoulders and leading me past all those important-looking men.

Inside the office, I said, "Governor, I want my brother home."

"Harvey, so do I," he said. "I need him as bad as you do."

The Governor started dictating letters and making phone calls. In less than two weeks, Tom got off the train in Austin in his Marine uniform. His family and friends were happy to see him—and so was Governor Hobby.

In the passing years I have often smiled to myself, wondering what those important-looking men might have been thinking when the Governor came out and took a twelve-year-old caddie into the office ahead of them.

Life in the Mind

IN GENERAL I am not a television fan, but I do watch every bit of golf that is available on the tube.

I study the swings. I try to read the thoughts of the players. One thing that remains the same year after year is that the player who makes the fewest mistakes is the one who wins. It's the same with a golf teacher. The one who makes the fewest mistakes is the best teacher.

Sleepless, I stare at the ceiling when the lights are out. I do a lot of teaching at night. A lot of learning, too.

My First Lesson

GROWING UP AS A CADDIE, I learned to play golf by trial and error and by copying the swings that I saw and liked.

The first lesson I ever had, I was already head pro at Austin Country Club.

My teacher was Walter Hagen.

We were playing an exhibition. I half-topped a couple of shots, and Hagen said, "Harvey, you want a word of advice?"

"Sure."

"You're trying too hard to keep your head down. Let your head be a little more free. Don't fall for this turn-in-a-barrel nonsense with your head fixed solidly in the center of your turn. You've got to move a little bit sideways along with your turn. This gets your weight onto your right foot and your head well behind the ball, so you can put power into your blow. It's like throwing a punch."

I took Hagen's advice, and I still teach that way.

Many times over the years I taught at PGA schools with great players like Paul Runyan, with whom I disagreed about the swing. Runyan was a turn-inside-a-barrel player and teacher, but a notoriously short hitter. I felt Paul could have profited from a freer swing, as Hagen had taught me. However, Paul won two PGA championships and was elected to the Hall of Fame doing it his own way.

As I see it, all those PGA schools were like golf lessons for me. I especially liked listening to teachers who taught differently than I do. They made me think.

Also, I learned afresh each year when a new class of golfers came to our team at the university. Each of these youngsters had learned to play from someone—a pro, a friend, a relative, a caddie. In getting to know our new players, I learned whatever they had learned.

Some of the best tips I ever heard came from small-town club pros like Hardy Loudermilk from Jal, New Mexico. Hardy is the fellow who sent me a young pupil named Kathy Whitworth.

When people ask who my teacher was, I say, "Everybody."

But I always remember that first lesson from Walter Hagen.

A Soft Wedge

A SOFT, FEATHERY WEDGE shot should be hit a little back of the ball, because the sole of the wedge is about an inch thick.

The tail end of the wedge must strike the turf behind the ball to get the ball flush on the face of the club.

This shot doesn't have the crisp feel, but I think with practice it produces good results.

The Examination

PAULA GRANOFF, my friend and pupil from Providence, went to Boston to have her eyes examined by a famous specialist.

Inside his office, the doctor asked her, "Are you the woman who takes lessons from that fellow in Texas and won your state senior championship?"

Paula said yes.

"Would you do me a favor?" the doctor asked.

Paula said she would try.

The doctor picked up a golf club that had been leaning in the corner.

He said, "Before I examine your eyes, Mrs. Granoff, would you please check my grip?"

Club Fitting

IT IS IMPORTANT THAT your shafts be the right length and flexibility.

The correct length is determined not by your height, but by how far your hands are from the ground. Regular-length clubs, just as they come from the manufacturer, will fit nearly everyone.

Flex of the shaft is a matter of strength and swing speed. Too often I see players who have reached middle age or beyond and still try to swing stiff shafts in the mistaken belief they will hit the ball farther. Softer shafts will give better results.

In the matter of the lie of the clubface, the average player should stick with what the manufacturers have made.

If you bend your club to make it more upright, you are going to throw a hook into your shot. If you flatten it out, you are building in a slice.

If your ball were to be sitting always absolutely level, as it is on the practice tee, the lie of the clubface would be very important.

But on the golf course, your ball will come to rest in all sorts of different situations—downhill, sidehill, uphill. You can't go bending your club to fit each slot.

The Best Hands

HENRY COTTON HAD the most stylish hand-action through the ball that I ever saw on a man. He was a stylish fellow all around—handsome, outfitted by London tailors, and he drove a Mercedes roadster. Cotton looked like the sort of player you would expect to win three British Opens, as he did.

Cotton swung the club with his hands. His body *followed* the action rather than *led* it.

His hands went straight down the line after the ball with a tremendously fast crossing of his forearms.

Cotton's swing looked lazy until he neared the ball, and then it was a blur, seemingly without effort.

Later a popular method of hitting the ball was the "quiet hands" school, in which the big muscles of the legs, hips, and back took over the job of hitting the ball, and the hands merely held on to the club.

Now I believe some players—like John Daly—are learning to use both the big muscles and the small muscles, but I haven't figured out how they do it. I wish John Daly would stop by and let me watch him hit a few.

When I consider all players, though, I would have to rank Henry Cotton second. Don January might be third. But Mickey Wright's hand action is, to my eye, the best ever.

I can't take credit for it. Mickey was already a finished player when she came to me.

She had been taught to feel as if she were holding a basketball between her knees at address. In her turn back, she rolled onto the instep of her left foot rather than lifting her left heel. Like Cotton, her hands looked slow and lazy until they approached the ball, and then they became a blur. Her wrists held their release until the last instant, and her left forearm rolled over with a tremendously fast snap.

One afternoon I asked Sandra Haynie to come watch Mickey hitting balls.

Afterward, Sandra told us both, "I like everything she does except the way she keeps her knees tied together at address."

Mickey just smiled pleasantly and said, "Well, I'll think about not doing it anymore."

But Mickey kept on with it and won eighty-two tournaments.

I wish all kids could learn Mickey's golf swing and be blessed with her personality.

A Hard Job

I WAS VISITING at another club, and I heard someone say to a member, "You really have a nice golf course here."

The member replied, "Yes, we're just one greenskeeper away from having a great golf course."

Greenskeepers have a hard and thankless job. They get blamed for things that are beyond their control, like the weather. If a club allows more rounds of golf to be played than the course can stand, the greenskeeper gets the blame for the bad patches.

There is no way a greenskeeper can please the good players, the average players, and the bad players all at the same time.

Mr. Aminex

WE HAVE A CLUB MEMBER I call Mr. Aminex.

The reason for this is, he never arranges a tee time. He just comes to the course. As the other players are teeing off, he keeps coming up to me and saying, "Hey, Harvey, am I next? Am I next?"

I usually reply, "Mr. Aminex, I looked under the Starter's Rock and didn't find anything, so you are not next."

The reference is to a club I heard about in California where the starter keeps a rock near the first tee. If someone shows up without a tee time, the starter looks under the rock. If the starter finds a fifty-dollar bill, a tee time is magically set.

We've never had a Starter's Rock at Austin Country Club. If we did and I found any money under it, I would probably faint.

One thing I would know for sure is that Mr. Aminex hadn't put the money there.

An Inexhaustible Subject

BOBBY JONES SAID he wrote half a million words on golf and nowhere near exhausted the subject.

He said, "I cannot imagine that anyone might ever write every word that needs to be written about the golf swing.

"In reality there is only one sequence of movements which is entirely proper in playing a golf shot. I have the conviction that no means will be found in the future of altering the effectiveness of this sequence within the limits imposed by physical peculiarities."

In the introduction to his classic book *On Golf,* Bobby explained why one sequence of movements should require legions of teachers and libraries full of books.

"The player must have the feel of the proper stroke. Yet the words in our language to describe feel are necessarily vague and susceptible to varying interpretations. No one can describe the feel of a muscular action with assurance that the description will be readily understood by another.

"For this reason I think it is necessary in all forms of golf instruction to repeat over and over descriptions of the same movements. Often the student will grasp the teacher's meaning when stated one way when he has failed to understand it in many other forms.

"Obviously, this procedure can result in almost endless discussions and speculations, but that is just the kind of game golf is."

A Tip

SHORTER PEOPLE usually do better if they address the ball on the toe of the club.

The Fee

ALL THROUGH MY TEACHING LIFE, people have said I don't charge enough money for lessons. They kid me about it. There is a story going around that Michael Jordan, the basketball star and golf lover, phoned and asked me how much I would bill him for a lesson.

Supposedly I replied, "It's five dollars an hour, and you have to pay for your own range balls."

This didn't really happen—at least, it hasn't happened yet—but people seem to want to believe it. I don't know what I might charge Michael Jordan for a lesson. Probably nothing.

I spent several hours on the practice tee recently with Ernie Banks, and that's what I charged him—nothing. I thought of it as a pleasure for me.

People phone the club or phone Helen from all over the world and want to come to Austin for a series of lessons. But I don't teach lessons in a series. I can't promise more than one, and maybe not even that much. It depends on what I think is needed.

I might take a look at a pupil and say, "Move the ball up." Or I might say, "Don't change your swing." How could I charge a fee for that?

A teacher's real reward is not money. It is the joy of helping others.

Timing

One question I am usually asked at teaching seminars is, "What is timing, and is it different from rhythm and tempo?"

Timing is getting your muscles together to produce the maximum speed of the clubhead at impact and the angle of face square on the line to the target.

Rhythm and *tempo* are words I avoid. They are not the same as *timing*.

There are plenty of good players who jump around during their swings, but meet the ball on the clubface at the right instant and get excellent results because of their timing.

The last player I wanted on my golf team was one who had to look good and have the prettiest swing without getting comparable results. Too often this player is satisfied with hitting stylish shots. Give me the player who is more concerned with putting the ball in the hole in the fewest strokes.

I know players who say they count in their heads—*one, two, three, four*—during the swing to help their rhythm or tempo. I don't see how they do it. If my mind is counting, how can I be taking dead aim?

Time to Move

I WAS WALKING through the airport in Atlanta when I encountered a friend, a famous golf pro from a famous club in Chicago.

"What are you doing here?" he asked.

"Teaching a seminar for the Georgia PGA," I said. "What are you doing here?"

"Changing planes. I'm going to Florida to look for a job."

I was surprised. "I thought you had one of the best jobs in the world."

He said, "I did, Harvey—until I agreed to serve on the handicap committee. I lowered a member's handicap by three strokes. The member caught me in the parking lot and said, 'Give me my three strokes back. I've had people killed for less than what you did, pro.'"

My friend packed a suitcase, and now he was on his way to Florida. I agreed that it was time to move.

Mr. Roberts

During a practice round at the Masters, the players were hitting fliers out of the fairway. One of my Texas boys, Terry Dill, complained to me about it.

I knew what was wrong. They had just started using winter rye in the fairways at Augusta, and I had watched them mowing the fairways with a rubber-tire tractor going about 30 miles an hour.

The rubber tires mashed down the grass instead of cutting it uniformly. After the tractor passed, the rye grass would spring back up and leave flier lies.

I told Terry that I had faced the same problem at Austin Country Club. My solution was to use steel wheels instead of rubber tires.

Terry said, "I'm going to go tell Mr. Roberts."

He meant Clifford Roberts, for many years the stern and somewhat autocratic boss of the Masters. I begged Terry not to go tell Mr. Roberts what I had said. But Terry is a headstrong fellow. He walked away from me, looking for Mr. Roberts. I felt like hiding.

Terry came back and said Mr. Roberts had gone to the barn to see the greens superintendent.

About ten minutes later here came the mowers again, and this time they had steel wheels and were moving slower.

Even though he acted on my suggestion, I stayed away from Mr. Roberts. I didn't want him to think I had come to his tournament to offer him advice on how to run it.

Randy's Driver

I HAD A PUPIL, Randy Mueller, who wanted to be the longest driver on the Austin High School golf team. I tried to persuade him that he should attempt to be the best player, not the biggest hitter.

I gave Randy a 2-wood and suggested he use it off the tee.

"I want to pull out my driver, the way the rest of the guys do," Randy said. "Pulling out a 2-wood on the tee is just not exactly cool."

I said, "We can fix that."

I took the 2-wood out of his hands, put a piece of adhesive tape on the sole and wrote a large "1" on the tape.

"Now you have a new driver," I said.

It wasn't long before Randy won a high school tournament with his new "driver."

He learned that hitting the ball straight and being in the right place is much more important than being impressively long.

Jack Did It

THE MODERN ALL-WEATHER, slip-on golf club grip was invented by Jack Burke, Sr., when he was the pro at Fort Worth's Glen Garden Country Club—where Ben Hogan and Byron Nelson were caddies.

Jack took a regular rubber hose, cut it the proper length, slapped some glue on the club shaft, slipped the hose on, and trimmed it into a grip.

I was playing golf with Jack the first time I ever saw his new grip, which was truly an innovation in the golf business.

Before then, it was hard work to put a good leather grip on a club. You had to wind strips of leather onto the handle just exactly right and then glue them tight. To remove one of those wound leather grips, you had to scrape and sand and file.

But with Burke's grip, you could pop it on or off in five minutes. It changed the lives of all golf pros.

The Downhill Lie

THE MOST FEARED FAIRWAY shot for the average golfer is the downhill lie.

A common mistake I see is that the player will try to stand up too straight.

The way to address the shot is with your body aligned on the same angle as the slope. For a right-handed player, this means your body will be slanted to the left.

Be sure to have enough weight on your left side to keep your balance.

Play the ball back in your stance. Swing the club with your hands and arms. Avoid the urge to raise up until your clubhead is through the ball.

Tension is a major wrecker of the shot off a downhill lie. Remember that your goal with this shot is not power, but a solid strike.

Haunted

MY CLOSE FRIEND Dick Metz, Wild Bill Mehlhorn, and I were paired at a tournament. Dick drew me aside as we were warming up.

He said, "I have to warn you, Harvey. Bill is so nervous about his putting that he will insist on hitting first on every green to get it out of the way."

Bill Mehlhorn won twenty pro tournaments, played on the Ryder Cup team and was a top teacher, but he was always haunted by the feeling that he was the worst putter in the world.

People ask me, "How is it possible for a person to win twenty pro tournaments and believe he is the worst putter in the world?" All I can answer is, "That's golf."

Dana X. Bible was the wildest hitter of the golf ball that I ever saw. He was a star player in football and baseball, and he won national championships as coach and athletic director at the University of Texas. But he couldn't shift his weight to his left side in his golf swing, no matter how many years of lessons I gave him. It seemed to be a total contradiction. This talented athlete could run for a touchdown or hit a home run, but to hit a golf shot he had to tee up the ball.

Of course, he didn't try to hide it. If you were playing with him for the first time, he would say, "I am going to tee up the ball whenever I want to, and you may feel free to do the same."

164

Our fairways in those days were scattered with worm casts, which D.X. used as tees when convenient. He insisted upon hitting up on the ball. Changing him was beyond my power.

I think people inherit quirky characteristics that may never show up except on a golf course.

In Bill Mehlhorn's case it was the contradiction of a superior golfer's being totally terrified of putting.

Hogan Whiffs It

IT WAS A CHARITY MATCH. Morris Williams, Jr., and Ed Hopkins were teamed against Ben Hogan and me.

With a large gallery around the first tee and people lining the fairway, we were waiting for Hogan. At last here he came, staggering a bit, a crooked grin on his face, his cap slightly aslant.

I could hear grasps from the crowd. "What's wrong with Hogan?" people whispered. "Why, it looks like he's drunk!"

Hogan fell to his knees trying to put his ball on the tee. He struggled to his feet, squinted down the fairway, rubbed his eyes, lurched backwards. Murmurs from the gallery grew louder.

Ben took a mighty swipe at his drive and missed it.

He grunted. He waggled and knocked his ball backwards off the tee. A caddie replaced it. Hogan tried again and topped his drive about 50 yards.

Morris, Ed, and I hit decent drives. We marched down to Hogan's ball. Wobbling, Ben lashed at his ball and hit a big slice. His cap fell off. The caddie picked it up for him, and Hogan put his cap on sideways.

Finally we reached the green. Ben knocked his first putt some 20 feet past the hole. He was still away. His second putt again went 20 feet past the hole. The gallery was aghast. Staggering, Ben lined up his third putt—and somehow the ball dropped into the cup.

Retrieving the ball, Ben fell down again. I could see the dismay on the faces of the gallery.

Ben stood up, looked around at the people ringing the green, and broke into a big smile. He straightened his cap. He said to me, "Okay, pardner, it's up to you on this hole. I'll do better from now on."

Suddenly the gallery caught on. Everybody started laughing.

Hogan wasn't drunk. He was just putting on a clown act for the people. Bob Hope couldn't have done it better.

It's hard to believe for golf fans who have grown up watching the great Ben Hogan, stern and impassive, winning major championships, but when he was younger Hogan was a terrific entertainer and salesman with a wonderful sense of humor.

The rest of the way, Ben played that charity match as if it were the U.S. Open. The college boys beat us 1-up.

Few people remembered the result of the match, but everyone that day remembered Hogan on the first hole. They talked about it for years. It was a side of Ben that not many galleries ever had a chance to see.

166

Caddie-Yard Psychology

FRIENDS OF A LOW-HANDICAP MEMBER have asked me to speak to him about his behavior. He gets angry at them on the course, scolding them for making noises, rattling their keys, moving around. If they're doing it to needle him, it would make me mad, too, but I would take it out on them by trying my best to beat them at golf. It's no fun to beat someone who doesn't mind losing, but it is special to beat someone who tries to take advantage. However, scolding your comrades will cost you friends, as was happening in this case.

I haven't spoken to the member about this, because the member hasn't asked my opinion. I have heard enough reasons and excuses—sometimes I wonder if we understand the difference—to be called an amateur caddie-yard psychologist, and I know this member would not like anything I might say. He is listening too hard to the sounds of the world.

If I told him to take dead aim, he would think I was simpleminded. But taking dead aim means blanking out the sounds of the world. It can be an advantage to be a little deaf.

167

Where Is He?

I WAS ALWAYS so quiet that Jimmy Demaret told me I ought to wear some of his brightly colored outfits just so people would know I was around.

I liked the way Ben Hogan and Walter Hagen dressed—gray and black and brown and white.

My Prayer

THIS IS THE PRAYER I usually use before beginning a teaching seminar:

"Dear God,

We come to Thee with a prayer that the Holy Spirit will be with us for this meeting.

Help us to remember that very few professions have as much influence on people as the golf pro.

Guide us and direct us in Thy way of life, that this will be a better world because we have lived in it.

Amen."

Training Aids

ALTHOUGH I TEACH a natural swing, I have made use of training aids. One of my favorites was a club that had a rubber hose for a shaft. You had to have a smooth swing to use it. Another was a chain with a grip on one end and an iron ball on the other. I could hit a golf ball 150 yards with that contraption, but I quit using it when the cotter pin came loose one day and the iron ball flew off down the range. It could have killed somebody.

I had a special golf grip—with grooves for the thumbs and fingers—put on a weed cutter. But I quit using the grooved grip because grips are such an important and individual matter.

Now and then I would get a pupil who was so wrapped up in hitting the ball that tension took over and he couldn't make a free swing at it. He might have a fine practice swing, but when you put a ball in front of him, his swing broke into pieces.

One fellow I remember would swing the club back all right, but when the club started down toward the ball he would freeze for an instant, then make a slash at the ball.

What this fellow thought he was doing was "pausing" at the top of his backswing. Tommy Armour taught his pupils to pause, which was about the only golfing notion

169

I disagreed with Tommy about. I don't believe you can call it a swing if you are going to stop in the middle of it.

This fellow I am speaking of didn't pause at the top, anyhow. He came to a dead stop on the way down with his hands about shoulder high. He had been a good player before this quirk overtook him. In an effort to cure it he sought out a number of teachers and even had himself hypnotized.

His practice swing looked like it belonged to the scratch player he once had been. But his playing swing looked ridiculous. He was so embarrassed that he was ready to give up the game.

I rounded up some thumbtacks and fishing line. I cut the fishing line into ten-foot strips and attached the strips to golf balls with the thumbtacks.

I would put a golf ball on a tee and tell this pupil to swing at it.

Sometimes I would jerk the ball off the tee with the fishing line before his clubhead reached it. Other times I would let him hit it.

The point was, this pupil never knew whether the ball would be there or not. It did him no good to worry about the ball during his swing.

Gradually he began to loosen up and make his practice swing at the ball, which was what I was trying to accomplish.

Necessity

A GOLFER rarely needs to hit a spectacular shot unless the one that precedes it was pretty bad.

Summing Up

EVERYTHING I SAY and do in my teaching is trying to produce these three things:
    Path of the club.
    Angle of the clubface.
    Clubhead speed at impact.

Game of Honor

GOLF IS A GAME of honor. If you are playing any other way, you are not getting the fullest satisfaction from it.

Observing the customs of honor should be so deeply ingrained that it never occurs to you to play dishonorably.

There have been countless examples of players calling penalty shots on themselves for violations that no one else saw—and in some cases losing tournaments because of it.

During the third round of the Kemper Open in 1993, Tommy Kite was leading and was paired with Grant Waite of New Zealand.

Near the fourth green, Waite took a drop from a Ground Under Repair area. As Waite prepared to hit to the green, Tommy looked over and noticed Waite's heel was still inside the Ground Under Repair marker.

This was a tournament Tommy wanted very much to win. It was his first strong showing since a back injury in the spring. It would have been so easy to glance away and pretend he hadn't seen where Waite was standing.

That is, it would have been easy for some people. For Tommy Kite, it was not even a consideration.

"We don't need any penalties here," Tommy said, pointing out the location of the New Zealander's heel.

If Waite had hit that shot, it would have been a two-stroke penalty. The penalty would have put Tommy in the lead by three. But, as I said, Tommy never gave it a thought.

Tommy said, "It would be pretty chicken for me to stand by and watch a guy accidentally break a rule and then say, 'By the way, add two strokes.' That's not golf. That's other sports where guys are trying to get every advantage they can."

Waite won the tournament by one shot. Tommy finished second.

I think I'm more proud of Tommy for that tournament than I am for his U.S. Open victory. An Open champion is a winner on the golf course. A person of honor is a winner everywhere.